DESIGNING
AND MAKING
GLASS JEWELLERY

DESIGNING
AND MAKING
GLASS JEWELLERY

Mirka Janeckova

THE CROWOOD PRESS

First published in 2019 by
The Crowood Press Ltd
Ramsbury, Marlborough
Wiltshire SN8 2HR

www.crowood.com

© Mirka Janečková 2019

British Library Cataloguing-in-Publication Data
A catalogue record for this book is available from the British Library.

ISBN 978 1 78500 677 7

Photographs by Mirka Janečková except where specified otherwise

Frontispiece: *Glass Drops* necklace, Mirka Janečková.

Acknowledgements
This book couldn't have been brought to life without the help of many people. I want to say a big thank you to all the wonderful artists who allowed me to use their images in this book – it would have been a boring book without you! Big thanks to my colleague David Mola for his specialist advice and huge help, especially with explaining copper foil technique. I am grateful to all the people from whom I learned about glass over the years – Petra Hamplová, Martin Rosol, Kristýna Fendrychová, and the teachers and technicians at RCA's Jewellery & Metals and Glass & Ceramics Departments and the Glass & Ceramic Department at the University of Wolverhampton where I was an Artist in Residence at the time of writing this book. I am very grateful for the awards from the Association of Contemporary Jewellery and the Edinburgh Council, which meant I was able to have dedicated time to explore and write outside my normal working and teaching schedule. Thanks also go to my studio buddy, photographer Brenda Rosette, for helping me with the images.

And special thanks go to all the family and friends who were so patient with me during the writing process.

Photos and sketches in this book are by the author, unless otherwise specified.

Typeset by Jean Cussons Typesetting, Diss, Norfolk

Printed and bound in India by Replika Press Pvt Ltd

CONTENTS

PREFACE

I am a jeweller originally from Czech Republic but now living in Edinburgh, Scotland. When I started my training as a jeweller I was fascinated by the properties of the metals involved and wanted to learn as much as I could about these, but later I wanted to add some different elements to my work. The first material I explored was porcelain: this is an amazing material with huge sculptural possibilities but what I was missing was transparency. I wanted to use material which could transmit the light. I was considering using plastics but they just didn't feel satisfying and precious enough. So my next choice was glass.

I started to work with glass in jewellery during my MA studies at the Royal College of Art in London. At that point I didn't know anything about how to work with glass so I searched for guidance in the literature. All the books I was able to find at that time were very technical, not that suitable for jewellery, and it looked as if a lot of strange, expensive equipment was needed to do even basic things. It scared me a bit but eventually I learned how to work with glass with the help of many people and with much of my own experimentation. And I fell in love with this beautiful material. A few years later, I thought that it would make sense to write a book which would help other people to enter the amazing world of glass jewellery and which would be easy to follow and understand – the book which I needed as a student years ago. This is it and I hope you will enjoy it!

LEFT: **Subterranean Rivers, Mirka Janečková. One of my first glass pieces from when I was studying at the Royal College of Art in London: I was experimenting with ways of casting findings such as chains directly in glass.**

INTRODUCTION

Glass is a fascinating material which has been part of our material culture for a very long time. It is one of the earliest man-made materials: some sources say that the use of glass by humans dates back over 5,500 years.[1] The earliest glass items found were small objects such as beads, amulets and statuettes.

From a jewellery perspective it is very interesting that early makers were using glass to mimic precious and semi-precious stones such as lapis lazuli or turquoise, or even precious metals such as gold. However, at that time, glass was not seen as a cheap substitute but as a material of equal value to the real gemstones. In ancient Egypt the glass was poetically called the 'stone that flows' and was seen as a luxury material, evidenced by the fact that most early glass was found in places such as temples, palaces or richly equipped tombs.[2]

Later, the knowledge of glass forming spread from the ancient kingdoms of what is now called the Middle East to the Roman Empire and then to other parts of Europe – Italy, Germany, Bohemia and as far as Britain and parts of Asia. The use of glass in jewellery has continued uninterrupted until the modern day but has flourished particularly in specific places.

One famous example is the Italian island of Murano which has been especially well known for its lampworking advancements (among other glassmaking skills) since the thirteenth century CE. The Venetians grouped all their glass manufacture on one island to keep the rest of the city from the potential fire risk but also to protect their advanced glass technology from being stolen and copied.

Another glass jewellery centre in Europe is Northern Bohemia (now Czech Republic), well known for manufacturing glass jewellery and beads from about the eighth century CE. Small seed beads from Bohemian factories have been used in tribal costumes as far away as Africa and North America.

Glass technology has continuously developed and invented; for example, lead glass with its brilliant shine was developed in seventeenth-century Britain. With industrialization in the nineteenth century, glass become more affordable and was not seen as a luxury item any more. Its manufacture spread over the whole of Europe, America and further.

In the twentieth century we can see the renaissance of hand making in the rise of the Studio Craft Movement. Many artist jewellers started to employ glass in their work once again. In this book I will be introducing the contemporary generation of jewellers who are using glass in their work to show the variety of approaches. It is exciting and satisfying to see that glass has been an inspiring material for jewellery artists and craftsmen for thousands of years and continues to be so.

LEFT: *Aventurine Green Glass Bubble Multilink Silver Neckpiece*, Charlotte Verity. (Photo: Charlotte Verity)

How to Use this Book

My main motivation for writing this book is to make glass techniques available for everyone: for people with no experience of making, for jewellers who want to employ a new material in their practice and for glass makers who want to learn how to use glass as a wearable item. I have done my best to explain all the glass techniques in a way which is easy to follow.

At the beginning of this book you will find out a little about the history and use of glass in jewellery through the ages. Then we look at the different properties of glass: there are various kinds, each of them suitable for a different use. This knowledge can then help you with your design decisions. In the chapter about designing we look at the designing process and

the challenges and specifics of using glass for jewellery purposes. This chapter also includes a brief introduction to glass techniques (hot forming, cold forming and decorative techniques). This overview may help you to decide which technique will be the most suitable for your design.

Detailed explanations of glass techniques are discussed in the next few chapters. In the two chapters on hot forming we will look closely at using kiln forming techniques and then go on to lampworking. The cold-working chapter looks at various techniques of shaping glass in its cold form. The final chapter considers ways in which to embellish your pieces. Each technique is explained in words but there are also many photos, illustrations and visual guides.

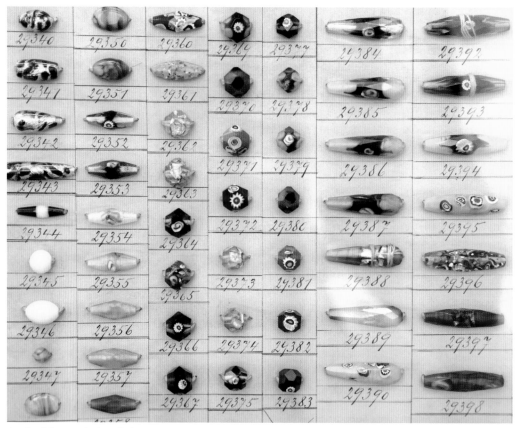

Card with sample beads from the collection of the Glass and Jewellery Museum in Jablonec nad Nisou, Czech Republic, where costume jewellery making has a very long history.

To really understand jewellery, glass or any making technique it is not enough just to know it in theory. It is a good start, but then it is necessary to start practising and gain direct experience of working with the material. There are two levels of knowledge in the making process: the first is to know something in your head (reading this book will help you with this); then there is 'the intelligence of your hands', which is gained only through practice. This applied knowledge requires you to be physically involved in the making process. You need to acquire both levels of understanding to be able to successfully create your pieces.

I would encourage you to try things, keep practising and don't be discouraged if something doesn't go well at the beginning. Glass is one of the most beautiful but also the most challenging material I have ever worked with.

Once the glass is broken it can't be 'fixed' like, let's say, metal. When something goes wrong it is usually better to start again from scratch. But the sense of achievement if something goes well is definitely worth all the struggle.

There are so many more exciting glass techniques to be discovered but for the purpose of this book I decided to choose simpler ones and especially the ones which are appropriate for smaller-scale jewellery making. So I will be omitting hot glass and some complex casting techniques as it would be unrealistic for a beginner to use these. If you fall in love with glass (and I am sure you will if you try a few projects), please keep learning and experimenting. I am attaching further literature at the end of this book for your reference.

I hope that this book will be an inspiration and encouragement to all readers.

GLASS AS A MATERIAL

Glass is a fascinating material unlike any other on earth. It does not fit into any of the three states which we use to describe our material world – solid, liquid or gas. Scientists have had to name a fourth state of matter for glass, calling it 'supercooled liquid', which means that glass keeps some properties of its liquid state even when it appears hard.

Science does not qualify glass as a solid because it lacks the crystalline molecule structure which is characteristic of solid objects. The inner molecules of glass are comprised of an open, unstructured and moving matrix. Most solid objects lose their crystalline structure when liquid but regain it when becoming solid but glass is the exception here: it does not have any crystalline structure, either when heated and liquid or when it is in its solid state at room temperature.

Heated glass actually never becomes fully liquid as, let's say, water. Even when reaching its highest melting point it keeps a toffee-like consistency. At this state, the glass is mouldable and can be used for all heat forming techniques.

Apart from the use of glass as an artistic material, it is widely used in domestic and indus-trial settings. For example, the ability of glass to transmit light is used in fibre optic broadband conductors, which can transfer information for long distances. Apart from its obvious use in architecture as windows, glass is used as an isolating material in science and medicine, as TV and computer screens or in renewable ener-gies. If you look closely around you, you will find that glass is practically everywhere in the urban environment.

You can find glass appearing in nature too; sometimes these 'natural' glasses are sold as gemstones. These can be obsidians, made of rock melted by volcano action (also called

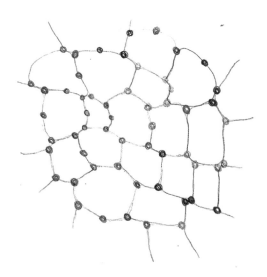

Sketch of molecular structure of glass. Glass has an interesting uneven crystalline structure unlike any other material, which is why it is classified as a 'glassy', not as a 'solid', state of matter.

LEFT: *Gummy Bears pendants,* Emma Gerard. (Photo: Emma Gerard)

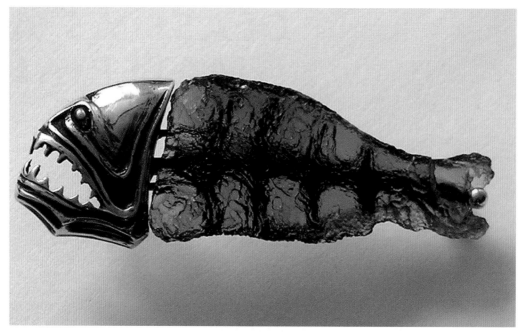

Fish brooch by Tomáš Procházka has a body made of Czech moldavite, a stone popular because of its intriguing story of originating from extraterrestrial forces. (Photo: Tomáš Procházka)

'volcanic glass'), or fulgurites formed by lightning strikes on deserts or beaches. Another interesting example comes from my home country, Czech Republic, and this is moldavite – an olive green gemstone which was created by the impact of meteorites crashing down on the earth thousands of years ago. These are still found today, often in the river Vltava – hence the name 'vltavín' in Czech. The real mineral is relatively rare but there are many fake ones cast from green bottle glass.

Glass has been man-made since ancient times and although the technology has advanced, the basic ingredients are still the same. Glass is made of about 70 per cent silica sand. The finely ground silica is then mixed with additional chemicals, such as soda ash, lime or lead, and heated together. Various oxides can be added to achieve colours. The liquid mass of glass can then be formed into a wide range of forms depending on what is needed – sheet, rods or ingots, for example. We will now look at the various types and properties of glass to help

you understand which kind of glass will be the most suitable for your project.

Types and Properties of Glass

As we have said, glass is made from heating and fusing silica sand with soda-lime (silica, sodium and calcium oxide), potash, lead, metal oxides or other chemicals. There are countless variations of this recipe, each addition giving the glass different properties, such as hardness, purity, electrical conduction or weight. It is not necessary to know the exact chemical composition of the glass but it is useful to understand which kind of glass is good for certain kinds of work.

Here are the main kind of glasses which are common in artistic practice, divided according to their chemical composition.

Crystal Popcorn Necklace, Petra Hamplová. Beads in this necklace were made by the lampworking technique, using soda-lime clear glass rods. (Photo: Petra Hamplová)

Soda-Lime Glass

This is one of the commonest types of glass and is used for manufacturing glass bottles, tableware and windows. It is suitable for most heat forming or cold forming techniques. There are countless variations in the glass with this composition – each manufacturer would have their own recipe.

Lead Glass

This is sometimes referred to as 'crystal' glass. It was invented specifically to maximize the reflection of light and is used whenever you need a great sparkle – for example, cut drinking glasses, chandelier elements, glass beads and crystals. The disadvantage for jewellery use is that the lead content makes this kind of glass a bit heavier.

Borosilica Glass

This is the hardest of the glasses used for artistic work. For this reason it is also used in the industry for making chemical and medical containers, light bulbs and oven-proof dishes. Its high durability gives it an advantage when making jewellery exposed to heavier use, such as bangles or long pendants. The disadvantage is that this kind of glass needs to be heated to very high temperatures to become work-able and there is a somewhat limited colour palette compared to other kinds of glass at the moment. However, this situation is changing as manufacturers are bringing new products onto the market all the time.

It is useful to know that there is a wide variety of different shapes and forms of glasses, each of which is good for certain techniques. Glass can take the form of sheets, rods, ingots or smaller decorative elements such as frits and stringers. There are also 'special' glasses which have specific optical properties, such as very clear colour effects.

Sheet Glass

This is especially useful for fusing and some cold forming techniques. It comes in different colours, transparencies and surface effects. The sheets are usually sold in flat form, but there are glasses with different patterns available as well.

The most common type of sheet glass is float glass: this is what you would know as 'window' glass. The name 'float' comes from the way in which this glass is manufactured. The liquid glass mass is poured onto large pans filled with liquid tin; glass 'floats' on the tin and later it solidifies and forms the sheet. That is also why window glass has always two different sides – tin and not-tin. Float glass comes in different thicknesses and sizes and is one of the cheapest options for your fusing or slumping projects. However, it is not usually compatible with other kinds of glass.

Glass for Casting

If you want to cast a transparent piece of jewellery then you need a chunk of glass. Glass for

Sheet glass comes in different thicknesses and a very wide variety of colours. Here you can see 3mm glass sheets with a CEO of 96, ready for fusing.

Various forms of glass ready for casting. For jewellery practice it is helpful to get smaller pieces of ready-crushed glass, otherwise you will have to cut or break bigger slabs yourself.

Lampworking rods come in a huge number of shades and effects. They can be transparent or opaque or 'special' ones with effects, such as alabaster or metal.

Decorative glass can be used in heat forming processes such as fusing or lampworking, perhaps on the surface of your pieces or as inclusions.

casting comes in slab, marble or round ingot form, depending on the producer. For the pâte de verre technique you use a granular glass called 'frit'.

Rods

Long thin rods are needed for lampworking techniques. They come in various thicknesses from 0.5 to 1mm. Some of them may contain several colours in one rod.

Decorative Glass

There is a very wide selection of decorative glass. Frit is a finely ground glass of various colours or colour combinations; stringers are very thin rods of glass used for decorative stripy surfaces; and confetti is comprised of thin shards of glass. The ancient decorative technique of millefiori (translated poetically as 'thousand flowers') is another option: this comes as patterned bead-sized elements with various intricate coloured patterns inside them.

These could be traditional flower patterns but also little animals or geometric shapes. You may be familiar with paperweights containing millefiori pieces enclosed in transparent glass form. All these decorative glass elements are particularly suited for fusing and lampworking techniques.

Special Glasses

If you are looking for some more unusual colour effects then you may like dichroic glass. These are glasses which appear to be multi-coloured. They change colour depending on the angle of your view and this effect is enhanced if the glass is used over a black or white background. They are made with a thin film coating technique and there is a variety of different effects available on the market.

Aventurine glasses have tiny metal crystals in them which create a sparkly shimmering effect. Some double helix glasses appear as lustrous metals. The market for special glasses is growing rapidly and manufacturers are introducing new effects all the time so check what is currently available. The selection may be a bit overwhelming at the beginning so I would advise you to think carefully about what kind of glass you need for your projects before you make your purchase.

Antique glass is a sheet glass mainly used for stained glass work. The difference from the normal sheet glass is that it is produced by the old and labour-intensive 'cylinder' method. This gives the glass a certain 'handmade' look which may be appealing for you.

Optical glass is clear glass of very fine quality. It should not contain any inclusions like bubbles or dirt. This would be the best choice if you want to work with optical effects or you are looking for a perfectly transparent material.

Working with Glass

So now you have learned about all these beautiful glasses which are available. But there are some limitations in how we can use the glass. First, it is important to consider the compatibility of the glass – the fact that two different kinds of glass can't be used together in the same piece.

Compatibility

Before attempting to join two pieces of glass it is essential to know their coefficient of expansion (known by the abbreviation COE). Unfor-

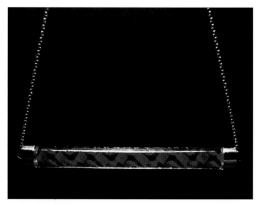

Photon Necklace, Yuki Kokai. This necklace was made from a hand-crafted glass rod mounted in 925 silver end caps and chain. The electric blue colour in this glass only appears when it has a dark background; it looks totally clear on a light one. (Photo: Yuki Kokai)

tunately it is not possible to use different kinds of glass together in one piece if each type of glass has a different COE. This is important to consider, especially in glass techniques which use heat processes such as fusing or casting.

Coefficient of Expansion

Glass, like most other materials, will expand when heated and contract when cooled. The speed at which this process takes place is called the coefficient of expansion and its value is different for every material and also for every type of glass.

If the coefficients of two types of glass are different, during the cooling there will be strain inside the material. The stress may not be visible to the eye at the beginning; cracking may happen during the firing or several months later. This could be tricky, especially if you have already sold the piece, or if your work is being exhibited. There is a device called a polarizer which would help you to identify the problem. Generally the glasses made by different manufacturers would probably have different coefficients so you wouldn't be able to use them in one project. The safest way is to stick with material from one manufacturer in one piece of work.

However, you can make a compatibility test by making a test strip. This may apply if, for example, you want to work with found glass or glass of unknown origin. Making a test strip is relatively straightforward. You place the different pieces of glass one on the top of another, then fire and anneal at the temperature you intend to use. After the piece cools down you can visually check for any cracks and then also use the polarizer filter to check for any problems invisible to the eye.

Compatibility: on this fused piece you can see a long crack on the surface. This sample was made with two layers of transparent float glass with red frit sandwiched between them to add colour; obviously the frit had a different CEO from the float glass.

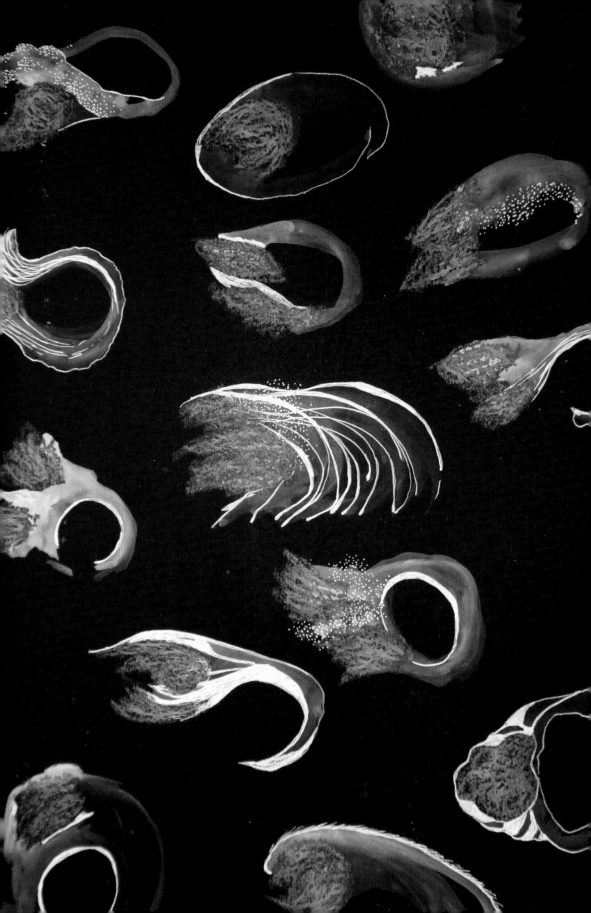

DESIGNING GLASS JEWELLERY

How to Start Designing

It is fine to look at the work of other artists or craftspeople for inspiration. You can examine such creations in books, magazines, museums or online. For centuries, copying the old masterpieces was considered the effective learning strategy across the world (although not so much now). This may be satisfactory for the start but after a while you may want to progress into realizing your own ideas. That is probably why you are reading this book. I believe that everybody has an inherent ability to source inspiration from their own interests, the things they like and the way they see the world.

Inspiration is everywhere. In order for your ideas to be authentic it is good to look at what you are already really interested in, what you like and what you find fascinating. It doesn't need to be anything art-related at all – the work may be actually more interesting if it is not. Do you like travelling, going to cinema, cooking or gardening? Great!

Once you have identified the area of your interest you will start looking more closely at its visual forms. At this point it is good to have some sort of gathering method. You can use paper, a sketchbook, boards, sticky pads, your phone, a 3D scanner or anything else. Start collecting images, photos, colour schemes and textures related to your subject. You may want to include little sketches of your ideas. It doesn't

LEFT: **Ring sketches by Mirka Janečková.**

matter if you think you can't draw; use line and colour to visualize ideas – it doesn't need to be a masterpiece. Think about it as recording pieces of information, like scribbling a reminder note to yourself. Nobody needs to see your sketchbook anyway. It is really useful to get into habit of recording every idea which comes into your mind. It doesn't mean you will actually make use of all of it but every little sketch can inspire you later on. Also, you may remember your ideas now but a week or a year later you may not. And it would be a shame to lose all that creative energy which is already in your head.

I found out during my teaching practice that people tend to take this initial designing stage too seriously. It is more helpful if you think about designing as more like playing. Most adults do not have the chance to play enough so this could be your opportunity. There are some really enjoyable methods which you can try. You can use photographs and magazine cut-outs, combining them and making collages. You can draw or paint over your photographs. Using transparent papers to trace random found shapes is always good fun. Combine different colours, materials and textures into one board and see how they interact with each other. Take picture of your arrangements, print the images and work with them further. If you like using your computer or your phone, there are many easy-to-use software packages you can use to create imaginative shapes and effects. Or you may want to work more conceptually and find adequate visual expressions of abstract concept or issues important to you. Try some of these and later on you may see that you are naturally finding your own way of working. Please do not

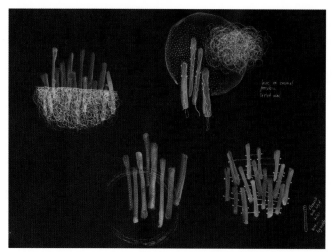

ABOVE AND BELOW: **Your sketchbook can be just a few scribbles in a notebook or on paper or it may take the form of free drawing. Sometimes I like to use black paper to visualize my ideas: drawing on black seems to be easier than on white for some reason.**

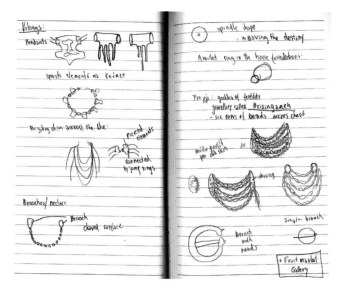

be possible to realize in 3D. Glass jewellery has specific properties which we will discuss later on in this chapter and these will affect your approach.

The next stage is to do some tests and samples: I would recommend to always do at least one test piece before you commit to investing resources into a final piece. You need to understand the possibilities of the material and technique you are using first. The more samples and test pieces you make, the better chance you have of creating a successful final piece.

Some people feel more inclined to skip the whole sketching part and go directly to the test pieces and samples. The inspiration then will come directly from handling materials and experimenting practically. The process itself is a good source of ideas and design possibilities. You can try both ways and see which one produces more fruitful results for you. The main thing is that you enjoy the whole process.

Glass has some unique properties, one of which is that it can behave slightly unpredictably. It is a material sensitive to a lot of outside conditions so a small change in your methodology can influence the results dramatically. There will be always the element of chance which actually makes working with glass so exciting. This is especially true about all kiln working techniques where you truly don't know what you have made until you open the kiln the day (or days) after. It is good to embrace this and use the unexpected results as inspiration for your further work. Some of the greatest pieces of art were made because something 'wrong' happened: the artist was wise enough not to dismiss this

judge any of your outcomes during this initial stage of the process: this is purely the exercise needed to generate raw material; the critical evaluation and technical execution will be required later on.

Once you feel you have enough visual material and start having clearer ideas of what you want to try in practice, then it is time to use your evaluation mind. Not all of your ideas will

as a mistake but look at the potential of such an event.

Now you are nearly ready to start making! Before we progress into technical explanations of the techniques I will discuss some specifics of using glass for wearable items.

Glass has very specific properties unlike those of any other material. There are a few things you must consider before you start making. We look at how to choose the right technique and finish for your project, at using colour and light and how to connect glass with other materials.

We will also look at things you need to consider when using glass for a wearable item.

Selecting the Right Technique

I divide the glass techniques described in this book into two categories. The first are described as 'forming' techniques: by using these you can

Using collage techniques, you can play with your photographs, drawings and writings and then include glass and other materials to create the 'mood' for your work and explore the textures involved. This is your visual research and experimentation, not a finished, neat project.

I like to keep all my test pieces in such boxes for future reference, even those which have obviously failed; they may inspire something else in the future.

actually create the desired shape from a mass of glass. The second group are 'decorating' techniques: these are the ones you use to embellish or finish the surface of your glass piece. Below, each technique is introduced so that you can imagine what is possible and then you can read the appropriate chapter later in this book. I would recommend you read the whole book anyway, as each piece of information can spark a new idea. In most cases, you will probably use a combination of two or more techniques in one work.

Heat Forming Techniques

Heat forming techniques are the ones which use heat to make a shape out of your glass. Depending on the temperature the glass may become soft or liquid and can take any form. For fusing, slumping, casting and pâte de verre

you would need to use a kiln so they are also referred to as kiln forming techniques. It is an indirect way of working: you prepare your glass and moulds before putting them into the kiln and then wait for the result. By contrast, with lampworking techniques you use a special glass torch to melt and shape the glass in the flame and so you can see the results immediately.

Fusing and Slumping

Fusing is probably the easiest of the heat forming techniques and may be the first one you try. Fusing is basically sticking two or more layers of glass together in the kiln to create a new shape. Most of the time you would use flat sheets of glass but it is possible to fuse other shapes as well. You can then work further with fused sheets of glass and form them into more 3D shapes with slumping techniques. In this case you lay down your glass over or inside the mould. The heat of the kiln will then cause the glass to 'slump' over or into the mould and take its shape.

Casting and Pâte de Verre

With casting you melt glass in the kiln until it becomes liquid. It can then take any form you define by using your moulds. You can make basi-

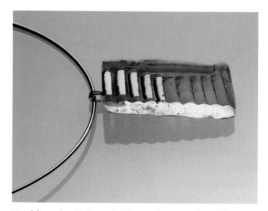

Necklace made from fused sheets of transparent clear and blue glasses. The loop findings were already fused inside the elements, which made it easier to assemble the whole piece.

Necklace by Deborah Timperley, made with pale copper blue glass, cast using a textured mould and combined with 23.5-carat gold sheet. (Photo: Nigel Frey)

cally any three-dimensional shape you can imagine with this technique. It is a little bit more demanding as you need to be able to prepare your moulds but the results are worth the extra effort.

Pâte de verre technique differs from casting in that you can easily create a hollow shape – this is really helpful for creating big but light pieces. Another advantage is that you can be more precise with placing your coloured glass in desired positions. You use a 'paste' of ground glass to create a layer inside your mould which is then fused together to create a solid piece.

Necklace for the Nymph, **Petra Hamplová. Both solid glass beads and empty glass bubbles have been used to showcase the artist's skill in making lampworked beads. (Photo: Petra Hamplová)**

Lampwork

This is the technique for people who prefer to see the results of their actions immediately. You use a special glass working torch (also referred to as a lamp, hence the name) to melt glass rods directly in the flame. By manipulating glass by hand movements and tools you can create a small-scale glass work. It is very often used for creating glass beads but the use of this technique is much wider.

Cold-constructed piece by Pavel Novák. Clear glass has been cold-worked into geometric segments; these are bonded together with coloured glue (in this case yellow), creating fascinating optical effects. (Photo: Pavel Novák)

Cold Forming Techniques

You may choose to work with glass without melting it and make your pieces using so-called 'cold' forming techniques. You can shape the glass by removing the material in different ways and then use different bonding techniques (such as using glue or metal foil) to create new shapes. Or you may choose to work with existing glass elements – both found (such as beach glass) or bought (such as beads) to make your pieces. This can be as effective as using heat forming techniques but without the need to invest in a kiln or other specialist equipment.

Cold-Working

Cold-working is a term used for a different method of shaping the piece of glass. Flat glass is relatively easy to cut into your desired shape with a glass cutter tool. If you then want to refine your glass even further, you would need one or more abrasive tools, such as a grinder, lathe or pendant drill. For achieving a shiny surface after you have worked on it, you will need to spend time on polishing your glass. Once you are happy with the shape of what you have created, you can either use it on its own or use some of the bonding techniques to join your pieces together. This could be using glue, setting or metal foil technique.

Metal Foil Technique

This is the technique traditionally used in 'Tiffany' lampshades and decorations but it is possible to use it for small-scale jewellery. The principle is similar to the traditional stained glass technique, only you are usually joining flat pieces of glass with metal (mostly copper) strips instead of lead frames. You can cut different shapes and colours, and place them next to each other to create mosaic-like shapes. Your first pieces will be probably flat but it is possible to build 3D shapes as well.

Found Glass

You don't have to always start with raw glass material. You can just use what is already available; for example, a found piece of beach glass. It has already a nice, round shape and matt finish so you don't have to bother with much cold-working. The only challenge would be how to make the piece or pieces into a wearable item.

Or you may find some interesting small pieces of glass at home, in a charity shop or at a local vintage market. The shape may already be right

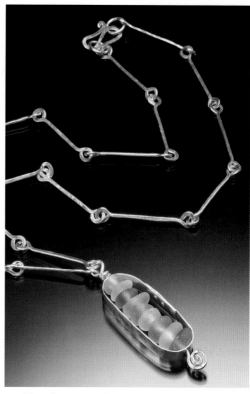

Necklace by Rex and Gene using found glass – in this case beach glass. The glass elements are drilled in the middle and held together by passing wire through the silver cage. (Photo: Guy Nicol)

for what you want to make. If not and the piece needs to be cut smaller or sharp edges removed, you can always use cold-working techniques to make it suitable for wearing. Please refer to the chapter on cold forming to find out more.

Decorating and Finishing

Once you have your glass shape formed you may want to work on it a bit further. Maybe you would like to add some colours, images or patterns, or perhaps create contrasting effects of matt and polished surfaces so let's have a look at suitable surface decoration techniques. Again, it is possible to combine two or more

Jewellery by David Mola using copper foil technique. Characteristic metal rims appear on the edges of the pieces but are also used as decorative elements to create the impression of stained glass windows. (Photo: David Mola)

Crystal Tags **by Klára Mikešová. She explains the inspiration behind these engraved pieces thus: 'Bohemian crystal glass, in the shape of army tags, refers to a Czech national identity. Variety of hand-cut decors is inspired from classic patterns, which have been used on Bohemian crystal glasses and beverage sets for centuries.' Winner of the Preciosa Master of Crystal Award 2016. (Photo: Preciosa a.s.)**

of these techniques to achieve the desired outcome. First, we will look at techniques which remove a thin layer from the surface of your piece, such as engraving, etching and sandblasting. Then we look at painting, printing on glass and using decals (transfers). Finally, we look at adding extra elements, either on the surface of your piece or in between the layers of glass as inclusions.

Engraving, Etching and Sandblasting

What all these techniques have in common is that they are based on removing a layer of material from the surface of the glass, each of them by different means. Engraving is the mechanical way – you are grinding material away by some sort of rotational tool. This could be a specialist glass engraving lathe or a pendant drill with diamond burrs. If you are looking for a more complicated design or a photo effect, or want to mass produce you may want to check laser or water jet engraving.

Etching is a chemical way of removing the material. An acid is applied on the surface of your glass. It will interact with the glass and 'eat away' the material until you wash it off. For creating a precise pattern it is helpful to cover the parts of your glass you want to leave intact with some sort of masking device.

Finally, sandblasting is again a mechanical way of removing material, only this time the work is done by a machine which uses a concentrated pressured stream of fine sand particles. The sand blasts away the surface of the glass.

The place where you removed the material from your glass will always have a matt surface. You can use this effect to achieve contrast in your work or this could be polished later on.

Painting, Printing and Transfers

Painting on glass is a good way of adding a bit of colour to your piece even if you have only one colour of glass available. You can achieve different effects with transparent or opaque paints. You can choose the paint to create the look of traditional stained glass or use only dark colours and white to achieve dark shadows and pale highlights; this latter would look a bit like

Natura Morte **by Philip Sajet is a good example of using glass enamel paint. The round painted glass is set into a metal frame to make a striking brooch. (Photo: Philip Sajet)**

a black and white photograph. There is a wide variety of special glass colours which could be fused on the glass permanently: these are called enamels. They are similar to metal enamels only formulated for glass.

And of course you can use semi-permanent glass paints which are fired at kitchen oven temperatures.

If you are not so keen on painting freehand you can try various printing techniques. You would use the same kind of paint, only applied by a printing method such as lino print, screen print or even shapes cut from potatoes.

Another option is to print your image or photograph onto a special transfer sheet, which can be placed on your glass and fired on. This is one of the easiest ways of using a photographic image in your glass works.

Surface Decorations and Inclusions

You may want to have a raised decoration on your piece of glass. This can be achieved by using smaller cuts of glass, such as glass strings (called 'stringers') or glass grains (called 'frit'). Then you have the option to fuse these pieces

ABOVE AND BELOW: *Palm Beach Shrub* necklace, Lisa Johnson. The glass element was achieved by complex fusing techniques. Lisa replicated the shrub imprint in green frit and fused it onto the clear glass, then set it an elaborate sterling silver and gold setting. (Photo: Lisa Johnson)

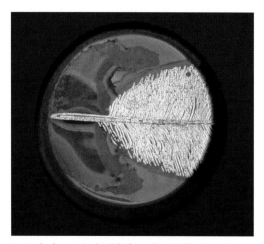

Brooch decorated with fused metallic transfer on the surface of a float glass circle. Transfers are basically stickers printed with enamel which can be permanently fused onto (or inside) your piece; you can buy them with pre-printed images or get them printed with your own image or photograph.

onto the surface permanently, in which case you would usually use fusing or, in some cases, lampworking techniques. Remember that the glasses would have to have the same coefficient of expansion. If you want to join two different kind of glasses you can always bond them together with (ideally) transparent glue. This would not be as clean or permanent a connection as with pieces fired on the surface but will work well if you use a good, strong glue.

Inclusions are another way to embellish your pieces. For this, you could use material like metal foil, thin wire, enamels or even air bubbles inside your glass. Note that at least one of the glass layers needs to be transparent so you can see the inclusions. You can use some of the 'hot' techniques such as fusing or lampwork to join the two layers of glass together. This connection will then be permanent and you will be able to work with that piece even further.

Alternatively, the cold way of bonding is called lamination and is mostly suitable when your inclusion are relatively flat. In this case you join the layers of glass with some sort of transparent glue, silicon or resin. Choose this method if you want to insert materials which would not survive heat, such as dried leaves, photographs, strings and so on.

Olive Beads **necklace, Petr Dvořák. Tiny crystals of Czech garnet have been set inside glass beads. The round shape of the clear glass beads makes the garnets appear magnified and slightly distorts their shape. (Photo: Petr Dvořák)**

Other Aspects

Light

Light is a factor which needs to be seriously considered when using transparent glass, less so when using opaque glass. Here are a few little tricks which will help you to use transmitted light to its full potential.

A colourful transparent fused pendant may look beautiful when it is held against a source of light but may appear dark and dull when worn on the body. It is because the clothes or skin are absorbing the light and don't allow it to be reflected back through the glass mass. This is something to watch, especially when using darker transparent colours or double layers. There is an easy solution for this problem and it is to add an opaque white or light-coloured glass layer at the back of your piece.

You can be a little freer while designing

This is my own piece *Czech Your Death*, made from engraved mirror, playing with the jewellery tradition of 'Memento mori' or 'Remember that you must die'. Memento mori pieces were made from the sixteenth century onwards but became very popular during the Victorian era. They served as a reminder of the fact that life is precious and nobody knows its duration so one must use it well.

earrings, especially long, hanging ones, as they hang in mid-air and reflect light easily.

Another fascinating property of transparent glass is that if you make it into round, concave or convex shapes, it will distort the objects placed behind or inside it. For example, if you make a round transparent bead with some opaque colour inclusion, the inserted shape will appear enlarged. The effect will change depending on the angle at which you view it: you can have a lot of fun playing with this.

You may decide to stretch the reflective quality of the glass even further and use mirror. Mirror is basically a sheet of transparent glass with a silver layer on the back. It is possible to work with a mirror in the same way as you work with a sheet of glass. You use only cold forming techniques as any heat will damage the silver layer at the back which creates the reflection. You can set mirrors by using metal foil technique or lamination. It is also possible to experiment with making your own mirrors by silvering the back of clear glass. Mirrors are fun to play with but they are also very powerful symbols in the human psyche and have been used in all sorts of spiritual and religious traditions across the world.

Colour

The first association for most people when you say the word 'glass' is an image of the clear transparency of window glass or maybe a glass bottle. But the beauty of glass is that it can have any colour you could possibly imagine. Apart from having all the colours of the palette avail-

able, there are 'special effects' glass: you can have metallic effect glasses which look like silver or gold, iridescent and dichroic glasses by playing with several colours in the same piece, or pearl and other luminous shades. And this is just to name a few. Glass can be opaque, translucent or transparent or any combination, and have matt or shiny finishes. There is so much choice it may sometimes be overwhelming when starting, so it is good to have a clear idea about your colour palette before you purchase your materials.

Colours can be added into glass in two ways – either the whole mass of the glass is 'stained' with different substances (usually oxides of metals) or the colour is added on the surface in forms of glass paints, lustres and enamels.

Coloured glass can be mixed together in hot processes as long as the materials have the same coefficient of expansion. When using cold assembly, you can freely mix any glasses together. Remember that you can optically mix colours by laying several layers of glass one on top of another; for example, if you layer yellow and blue sheet glass, it will appear as green.

If you like to experiment or if you want to achieve a truly unique palette for your work, you can try making your own colours by adding metal oxide powders into transparent glass. This is especially suitable for the pâte de verre technique as you can easily mix glass powder

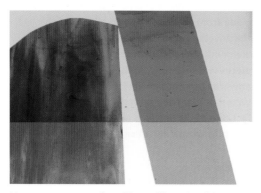

Here you can see the effect of layering blue and yellow sheet glass. You can use this simple mixing effect with your fused glass pieces. Remember that this will work only on pieces which can transmit the light, like earrings; otherwise you would have to use white background glass to bring the colours to life.

David Mola's experiments with fusing silver foil and silver dust on float glass. Once silver is fused it creates interesting yellow/gold layers. The more material is added, the greater the depth of the colour. (Photo: David Mola)

or frit with oxides. But you may try to experiment with other heat forming techniques as well or use oxides for painting on the surface of the glass.

Here is an initial guide on what sort of colours you can achieve, although, of course, this technique requires quite a bit of experimenting and testing. Please refer to specialist literature if you want to progress further.

Metal oxides:
Cobalt – light to dark blue
Copper – blue green or ruby red
Silver – yellow
Manganese – yellow/purple
Uranium – greenish, yellow
Iron – green
Selenium – rose, orange
Gold – ruby red to rose (that is why red glass was really expensive in history, now new technology helps you to achieve this colour)
Manganese – dark red

Other rewarding ways of adding colour to your work without the need to buy every shade is to use glass enamels, paints, decorative glasses such as frits or stringers, or slide-on decals or transfers. All of these can be placed on the surface of your glass or 'sandwiched' between two layers as inclusions. That way you can use just one basic colour of glass and achieve coloured accents by using these techniques.

Assembly

One of the main challenges in designing and making glass jewellery is connecting glass with other materials. To become a wearable object, glass pieces need some means of being attached to other items. There are several ways of achieving this.

Beads
The simplest way would be to use beads; that is, pieces of glass with holes through them. This

RIGHT AND BELOW: **Emma Gerard's playful pendants look very like gummy snake sweets. The hole for the chain is at the top of the piece and is created by casting, a simple but effective technique for turning your pieces into wearable items. (Photo: Emma Gerard)**

allows the use of different kinds of strings or chains to make the piece wearable, perhaps as pendants, neckpieces or simple bracelets. You can design the constituent pieces so that they each contain a hole, which would be the easier option. It is also possible to drill the hole after making, which is a bit more time-consuming. This latter approach may often be appropriate when some of your test pieces turn out really well and you want to use them further.

Findings
There is plenty of choice of findings available; it really depends on your taste and design concept as to which ones to use. You can have strings, chains, earring blanks, brooch backs, ring bases, tubes for beads – pretty much anything you can imagine. It is important to consider which materials your findings are made from. Some people may be allergic to non-precious base metals like zinc or nickel. Sterling silver,

Yuki Kokai's *Shore* earrings consist of two layers of clear glass enclosed by silver pendant settings with earring hooks. Trapped in between the layers are small glass balls which can move freely inside the piece. This is a really clean, considered use of custom-made metal findings. (Photo: Yuki Kokai)

gold and other precious metals are usually safe but be careful with 'silver-plated' or 'gold-plated' findings or those which claim they are 'silver or gold colour' or similar; these could be made of anything. If you are not sure, always check the hallmark. Hypo-allergic stainless steel findings are usually a safe choice.

As you may be a jeweller already then you may want to make your own findings. This is always the best choice as you are in control of the materials and you can make your findings to exactly match your glass pieces.

This piece has bigger metal elements cast in the clear glass. The chain is attached in the glass part of the pendant. With larger inclusions you would need to be more careful as glass can only absorb a certain percentage of foreign elements inside itself; test pieces are recommended.

Fusing Findings inside the Glass

Glass mass is capable of withstanding a limited amount of other materials inside itself. This property of glass can be used for inserting the jewellery findings and connection materials; any heat forming technique would be suitable for this. The material inserted has to be able to survive the fusing temperature (700–800°C depending on the type of glass). Most of the commonly used metals would fall into this category – copper, brass, silver, gold or other precious metals. There are also specialized findings made especially for glass fusing and sold by glass suppliers. It is essential to check the melting temperature of the metal; when this is higher than fusing temperature then the metal should be fine to use. Be aware that some silver-plated chains are made of aluminium or aluminium alloys which would melt at low temperatures. Also check that the wire does not have any plastic coating which could burn and possibly damage your piece and your kiln.

The number of insertions should be kept to a minimum. Too much inclusion would cause stress and then breakage of the glass during the cooling process. Judging the amount of material used may require a bit of practice as it is sometimes difficult to predict the outcome. There are many elements which could influence the process, such as the type of glass and metal, the temperature, the amount of glass compared to metal and so on. I would strongly recommend doing some test firings with any inclusions before making final pieces.

Bonding with Glue

This may not sound like the most sophisticated technique, especially for trained jewellers, but sometimes this is the most appropriate solution for joining glass with other materials.

There are different kinds of glues so the important factors you need to consider are mostly strength (the stronger the better), transparency and water-resistance. Two-part transparent epoxy glues are usually a good choice. There are special, very strong UV light curing glues which are recommended for bonding

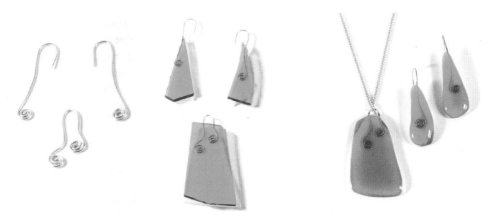

Fusing findings directly to the glass saves you from having to deal with attaching them later on. This is a simple example of how to fuse simple silver wire findings inside your piece to create earrings and a pendant. First you shape your findings with pliers; I have chosen a spiral motif. This part will later be fused inside the glass. Then I lay the glass sheets under and over the wires; here, I have used opaque white and transparent blue 3mm glass. Sometimes it may be tricky to keep the layers in position so use a little gum arabic to hold the pieces together until they fuse. The last picture shows the finished fused jewellery: the edges of the glass are rounded and the findings are securely attached. Remember not to use this technique in a microwave kiln; no metals should ever be used in a microwave

glass onto glass. Before using any glue, make sure that both of your surfaces are clean and dry, as moisture will inhibit curing. For the applying glue, always refer to the manufacturer's advice as each glue will be different.

In most cases you want your glue joint to be as invisible as possible. However, you may want to choose to use glue as a decorative element. There are specialist colour additives which can be mixed with your glue for this. The resulting effect will then appear more as a layer of paint rather than glue. This is suitable mainly if you are bonding two transparent glasses together or with other materials – it is another interesting way of using colour in your work.

Riveting

Riveting is one of the traditional jewellery techniques of attaching two materials together. The two most common ways are to use tube or wire. The wire will be inserted through the hole in both materials and then you use riveting tools to push the top of the wire over from both sides, thus securing two (or more) materials permanently together. You can make your rivets from scratch but you can also buy all sort of rivets pre-made. The advantage of this

Pavel Novák uses bonding with glue to its full potential in his cleverly constructed pieces. He uses cold-worked glass of optical quality combined with coloured glue to achieve interesting effects. This angular design reflects the colours of the bonding in the different facets of the piece depending on the angle of view. (Photo: Pavel Novák)

Bekkie Ora Cheeseman has used flat sheets of colourful glass in her sculptural necklace. The glass is cold-worked into round shapes which are then attached with rivets to the central silver pole. (Photo: Bekkie Ora Cheeseman)

technique is that you do not need to use any heat for bonding as compared with soldering. The disadvantage is that you need to be very careful applying the rivets as the impact of the riveting tool may break the glass. If successfully executed, this is a very clean, neat way of connecting glass with other materials.

Setting

Glass objects can be put into in metal settings in the same way that stones are set. However, you need to be careful – glass is not as hard as most of the stones traditionally used in jewellery. The hardness of the glass on the Mohs scale of hardness is somewhere around 5 (depending on the kind of glass). This is similar to some of the softer semi-precious stones. Setting glass pieces may be more challenging for the beginner as

I like to make my own metal settings by using the lost wax technique. This allows me to design bespoke shapes for the clasps and the whole ring. First, I make a ring model, including the claws, out of special jewellery wax; I make sure that the glass elements fit perfectly in the wax setting. Then I take out the glass 'stones' and send the wax model to be cast in silver. Once the metal part of the ring is back and cleaned, I set the glass in its position, pushing the metal claws and working carefully to avoid scratching the glass.

glass is more prone to break or scratch in the process of setting than harder gemstones such as diamonds or sapphires. But don't be scared – it is still relatively easy and doable, you just need to be more careful.

Most costume jewellery is made by setting glass crystals that imitate the cuts of precious stones; a good example would be Swarovski crystal. Historically, glass has always been used to imitate more expensive precious stones. On first glance, glass and gemstones can appear very similar.

Apart from the nearly unlimited design possibilities, setting glass pieces in metal has another advantage. The polished metals have the ability to reflect back the light coming through the transparent glass mass and in that way the glass becomes illuminated and the colours are clearly visible.

If you have a knowledge of jewellery techniques I would recommend you make your own settings as you can match them exactly to the shape of the glass piece. However, it is possible to buy ready-made settings from jewellery and findings suppliers.

Electroforming

Electroforming is another, less common technique used to connect glass pieces with metal.

With this technique you can 'grow' a layer of metal over your piece using an electric circuit. The basic principle is that you paint the surface of your piece on which you want to grow metal with special metallic paint. Then you create a circuit connecting your glass piece, your metal piece and a battery. Then you submerge the whole assembly in a conductive solution. When the electricity starts running through your circuit, the metal particles start covering the area of glass covered with metallic paint. The longer you leave the electricity running, the thicker the layer.

Copper electroforming is relatively easy and you can even buy the whole set-up ready-made from various suppliers. Electroforming using silver and other metals is more demanding as the ingredients needed for this are highly toxic; take professional advice.

Other Ways of Attaching Glass

You may find your own alternative ways of attaching glass to other materials. It could be all sorts of textile techniques like crochet or net making, or setting with plastic or wood, even stones. The pictures overleaf show some examples of interesting ways of assembling your glass pieces and combining them with different materials.

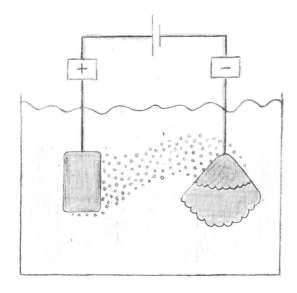

Schematic sketch of copper electroforming. A piece of copper (left) is attached with copper wire to the glass piece (right). The glass needs to be painted with conductive paint. Both copper and glass are submerged in special electrolyte solution. When the electricity starts running through the circuit, the copper starts to flow through the solution and deposit on the glass but only on the areas covered by paint; the rest of the piece will stay copper-free.

Private Messages, Caterina Zucchi. The artist uses string and pieces of paper to connect the whole necklace together. She explain the concept behind her piece: '*Private Messages* talks about what we cannot show and what we keep intimately protected within us. To access the content of the glass elements, they must experience a change that in this case is the breaking of the elements themselves. But, in contact with reality, will *Private Messages* be able to survive?'

In this neckpiece, Petr Dvořák is using a clever titanium mechanism to secure the glass and garnet beads and construct the piece. Here is how he describe his process and choice of materials: 'Garnets and glass are classic Czech materials that meld well. By using a metal-free technique to secure the garnet on or in glass, I achieve a new and unexpected effect that shows Bohemian garnets and their unique red hues in new splendour – in terms of jewellery an ideal combination. Titanium is a most practical material for jewellery design. It is as light as aluminium, but incomparably harder and more robust. Titanium can be used to create more voluminous structures which, thanks to the metal's durability, can stand up to any environmental corrosion. Titanium features one splendid property; it never tarnishes and its colour remains constant.' (Photo: Petr Dvořák)

Federica Sala has developed truly unique ways of involving stones and other unusual inclusions in her pieces. Here, she uses clear glass cast over the stones to create a brooch. She explains the ideas behind her work: 'I like glass to show all its contradictions. When transparent it disappears; when black it becomes liquid. It's delicate despite a chemical composition that belongs to the mineral world. It's multiform, viscous and solid, light and heavy at the same time.'

Hallmarking

This is a reminder for those who are not yet familiar with jewellery making. When any precious metal is used in your glass design there is a law which requires objects made of any precious metal (silver, gold, platinum) over a certain weight to be hallmarked. This means that the metal item has been tested and certified as genuine. This is done by stamping (or laser engraving) a small mark on the metal piece and this is called the hallmark. The hallmarking law is different in every country so you need to check the legislation which applies for you. For example, in the UK pieces can only be hallmarked in an Assay Office, not by individual makers as is common in other countries.

Metal suppliers also sell items, such as chains or clasps, that are already hallmarked. Some makers choose to hallmark all their precious metals elements even when they do not reach the weight limit, just to assure their customers of the provenance of their materials.

If you choose not to hallmark your pieces, you can still sell them, only you cannot refer to, say, 'sterling silver' as such; you should use the term 'white metal' or some similar term instead to comply with the hallmarking law.

Wearability

Designing an interesting piece of glass jewellery on paper is one thing but making it into a wearable piece is another matter. Not all your ideas may work in real life, but it doesn't matter – that is the way you learn and come to understand the challenges of the material. Here are a few tips on making your jewellery comfortable to wear.

Weight Limitation

As jewellery is worn on the body it needs to be comfortable against skin or clothing. As much as this is very individual and a personal choice there are certain weight limitations which make jewellery safe to wear for long period of time. This is especially true of earrings: people may have different preferences but overall it is not recommended for earrings to be heavier than 7g to prevent damaging the earlobes.

Thin Pieces

Very thin pieces of glass could look fantastic but they may not be safe for wearing. The thinner the glass, the more fragile it becomes. When glass is broken, the edges are in most cases very sharp and could easily hurt the wearer. You can solve this problem by creating metal settings around thin pieces of glass to add some strength to your piece.

Sharp Edges and Points

Make sure you remove any sharp edges from your glass pieces. It is very common to use diamond drill bits to remove unwanted bits while using heat forming techniques, such as fusing or casting. Any sharp bits left can hurt the skin, scratch the clothing or damage the findings. Also, be careful with the sharp edges of your beads; these can cut the strings, especially if you are using softer textile or leather materials.

Now you have learned enough to have a basic understanding of designing and making glass jewellery so it is time to dive deeper into individual glass techniques. In the next chapters you will find out more about heat forming, cold forming and decorative techniques.

HEAT PERFORMING TECHNIQUES 1: KILNWORKING

These techniques manipulate the glass by surrounding it with heat. We will be talking about fusing, which is probably the most accessible way for the beginner, then slumping, casting and pâte de verre. The essential similarity between these methods is that they all require the use of a kiln. We are not directly applying an open flame on the material as with lampworking (which will be discussed later) but rather using controlled temperatures inside the kiln to produce sufficient heat to change and influence the shape of the glass. In most cases, you will not have direct access inside the kiln during the firing as this will influence carefully programmed temperature timetables. It means that it is essential to correctly prepare your pieces and choose the right firing temperature before the process starts. Once the kiln is on you just have to wait and hope for the best. As Keith Cummings states: 'Opening the kiln combines the mystique of alchemy with the excitement of a lottery.'[3]

First, we look at the equipment for kiln forming techniques and some essential skills like preparation of the materials, cutting glass and the process of firing and its phases. This will be very similar for all the techniques. Then we progress to examine the various techniques in more detail.

Tools and Equipment

Cutting Glass

Glass is a hard but brittle material so we can use these properties when cutting. It is enough to score the surface of the glass to be able to break it easily. The process of cutting glass is easy but it requires practice. I would recommend practising cutting on some cheap float (window) glass first and then progressing to the more specialist materials once you feel confident.

LEFT: **Ring by Federica Sala. (Photo: Federico Cavicchioli)**

RIGHT: **Tools for cutting glass: glass cutter, grozing pliers, breaking pliers, cutting square, safety gloves.**

Here is a list of equipment needed:

- Glass cutter: the tool used to score the surface of the glass. If you will be cutting a lot of glass then it make sense to invest in better-quality self-lubricating ones.
- Grozing pliers: these have grooved teeth at the front which are used to nib the sharp edges and remove excess glass.
- Breaking pliers: these help to break glass after it has been scored. Some skilled people break the glass just with their hands but this may be a bit scary at the beginning so I would recommend using pliers.
- Cutting square: very useful for getting straight lines on your glass.
- Safety glasses: an essential piece of equipment as there may be small pieces of glass flying around when cutting and breaking glass.
- Cutting oil: not absolutely essential but this makes it easier to score and cut glass.
- Clean flat surface: this should be covered with something soft, like felt, lino or even layers of newspapers, to prevent the glass from being scratched.

When scoring the surface, for a straight line use the cutting square to support your line or choose to score freehand. The line should be scored in one continuous movement. It is not recommended to go over the scoring line again once you have stopped as this could cause the glass to break unevenly. It requires concentration and practice so that is why it is better to first try with scrap cheap pieces of the glass to gain more confidence. If you don't manage to get the line you want in one shot, it is better to start again on a different place or turn the glass on its other side and try again. Do the scoring while concentrating fully and apply steady pressure. Some people prefer to stand up while cutting glass so you may want to try this. While cutting you will hear a soft cracking noise – with experience you will learn to tell when something is not right by the quality of the sound.

After the glass is scored you hold the glass with breaking pliers (or your hands) and apply a little pressure at each side; the glass should break easily along the line. Be careful at this point as the edges of the glass will be very sharp. It is advisable to wear safety glasses, an apron and protective gloves while cutting.

While using heat forming techniques you will not need to do anything about the sharp edges as these will be melted anyway. Just be careful when handling it. However, edges could be ground or cut with a diamond saw if you want to achieve a particular shape. For this please refer to the cold forming chapter of this book.

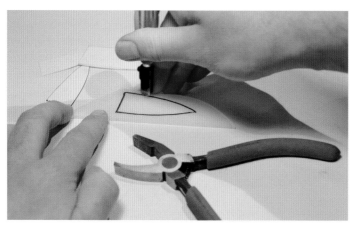

For freehand glass cutting it is helpful to draw the shape on the glass with permanent marker. Don't forget to clean your glass before fusing as marker can interfere with the heat processes.

Cutting Saws

If you want to cut a larger piece or if the glass is textured it is helpful to use a special cutting saw. Instead of metal, this saw has a diamond blade, which needs to be constantly lubricated by water. As an alternative to this specialist saw you could try a tile cutting saw as available from DIY shops; just check with the manufacturer's instructions that it is suitable for glass.

The first picture is a front loader kiln; this kind of kiln is a good all-rounder and can be used for casting, pâte de verre and other techniques. The second is a top loader kiln designed for fusing; it has the heating elements within the top lid, which helps to distribute the heat evenly.

Water Jet Cutting

If you want to cut very intricate patterns which would be difficult to achieve by hand or saw cutting you may consider using water jet cutting. This technology uses water under very high pressure and will cut through virtually any material, including glass. It is quite fascinating that water alone can have such a power. You will need to contact a specialist company to provide this service for you.

The Kiln

Buying a kiln is a significant investment but this is a piece of equipment which will last you for very long time and can be used for several glass techniques. If you are worried about the high initial cost you can start by using a basic micro-wave kiln, which is very affordable but has a limited use. Perhaps later you could progress to a more versatile programmable kiln.

There are many kinds of kilns available – some of them are specifically designed for fusing or casting, some of them are more versatile. The main guidance would be that the kiln needs to be able to reach the required temperature and have a controller which operates the tempera-ture (a microwave kiln would be an exception).

Kilns come in different shapes and sizes. They may be referred as front loaders (the kiln opens in front and the heating elements are usually on the sides) or top loaders (the kiln opens at the top). An example of the top loading kiln is the flat fusing kiln; this has heating elements on the top which help to distribute the heat more evenly. Ceramics kilns are perfectly fine to use for glass techniques as well; you just need to be

more careful with cleaning your kiln properly between each firing to avoid contamination.

The small kilns will run on the usual three-pin household electricity sockets but bigger kilns will need special electrical sockets, in which case it is advisable to get your electric supply checked and installed by a qualified electrician.

A kiln needs to have a controller that can operate the various heat phases, as the glass needs specific times to heat, hold or cool down. The controller reads the temperature through the thermocouple inside the kiln and manages the whole firing process.

Unfortunately, enamelling kilns are not suitable for glass techniques as their temperature cannot be changed during the firings to accommodate the different stages of the process.

Microwave Kiln

This is basically a box made from insulation material which intensifies the microwaves to create a high temperature inside. It can be used for small-scale fusing but this would be enough for most jewellery work. Be aware that you can't place any metal findings in the microwave. Please use separate microwaves for glass making and food to avoid any health hazards.

The glass is placed inside the kiln on a piece of kiln paper and the kiln is then placed inside the microwave. Then you switch the microwave on full power for three to fourteen minutes, depending on the size of your kiln (for a small kiln three minutes would be enough). Your kiln manufacturer will advise you on the exact timings. The heat generated inside the kiln should be enough to fuse the glass. You can lift the lid of the kiln very briefly to check the piece. Use heatproof gloves as materials inside the kiln will be glowing hot. If the glass edges are rounded then the glass is fully fused. Then you let your piece cool down naturally. Do not open the kiln during this stage as there is a danger of cracking. After thirty minutes to an hour, check if your piece is cooled enough to room temperature. Be careful while removing used kiln paper. You should wear a dust mask and gloves to prevent any irritation.

This method require some testing: as there is no temperature control you may not get good results immediately; keep a record of your firings as a reference. The more you use your kiln the more confident you will become. A microwave kiln is a good beginner's piece of equipment for basic fusing and small-scale slumping techniques. It is very easy to use and you don't need to understand the different stages, temperatures and times of firing – which could be quite overwhelming if you are just trying to make glass pieces for the first time. But after a while you may want to progress onto a larger kiln with a controller so that you can experiment with other techniques.

Firing Services

If you don't want to invest in buying your own kiln, it is possible to access firing services from glass studios or individual artists.

Preparing the Kiln and the Glass

Before you start firing, the inside of the kiln must be clean. Any particles left inside the kiln may affect the results of your firing.

You may be using some sort of kiln furniture inside the kiln. Kiln furniture allows you to stack more layers of your pieces into one firing and it protects the kiln in case something goes wrong. The kiln furniture needs to be covered with a layer of separator to prevent glass sticking to it; this is called kiln butt or kiln wash. It is basically

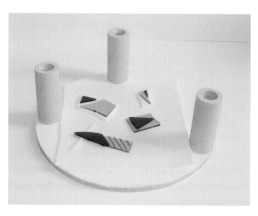

Kiln furniture: a round base and three columns ready, with a sheet of kiln paper. Depending on the size of your kiln you may fit more than one layer of bases, stacked on top of each other, to use the space as efficiently as possible. The firing temperature inside the kiln differs slightly depending on where your piece is – on the bottom, middle or the top. Normally it is not a problem, you just need to remember that if you do any experiments you must note the position of your pieces as well as the firing schedule.

a material which prevents your glass sticking to the surface of the kiln or the moulds when it is in its molten state. There are various ways of painting the butt but one of the most efficient is to spray the heated kiln furniture (at about 100°C) with a weak solution of separator and water. Water evaporates when sprayed on the heated surfaces leaving a nice, even protective layer.

Another easy way to protect the surface of your kiln is to use kiln papers. These are special papers made from ceramic fibre which are designed specifically for kiln forming techniques. They work very similarly to the kiln wash, only instead of painting or spraying the separator layer, you would simply put kiln paper on your shelf. Your glass can be placed directly on top of it. It is safer to wear protection gloves, glasses and mask while working with any material containing ceramic fibre. Using kiln papers is a little more expensive than using kiln wash as you will probably need to replace them after every firing but they are very easy and quick to use so it will save you time.

For certain projects you may need to use separators in different ways – as the devices which support or form glass during the firing. Their essential quality is that glass does not stick to them. Thus they can be used for making moulds, holes or forming the glass inside the kiln. An example of this would be inserting a bit of rolled kiln paper between two layers of glass to create a hole for a pendant.

Separators can also be made of metal, ceramic, powders, kiln wash, ceramic paper or plaster. Basically any material which can survive fusing and casting temperatures can be used as a separator. Metal sheets or rods are very useful for creating spaces for findings, holes and so on, but any metal must be covered by kiln wash or a similar separator, otherwise the glass may fuse onto it permanently.

Separators or moulds can be used to intentionally imprint pattern or texture onto glass. You may want to try mesh or perforated sheets of kiln paper placed underneath your project to obtain different imprint effects.

The glass needs to be really clean from any dirt or even fingerprints, otherwise the impurities may be permanently fired onto your piece. Use white spirit to clean your pieces before firing.

Kiln Processes

Annealing

It is very important to understand this part of firing process, which is crucial for any hot worked glass. If not done properly, the glass will crack: this could be after cooling down or even several weeks after the firing. This could have really unpleasant results; for example, if you have already sold the piece.

Let's have a look at what is going on inside the kiln during the firing. During the transition of glass from its liquid form to solid there is a lot of stress inside the glass caused by different speeds of cooling inside it and at the surface. When the glass is cooling it starts to shrink and harden but as glass is not a good conductor of heat it cools down unevenly. While the middle of your piece may be still hot and molten, the edges are already cooling and hardening, thus creating tensions and cracks. The same thing can happen during the heating period – the outside of the glass could already be heated and expanding while the middle is still cool and rigid.

Sketch of processes inside the glass when it is being warmed or cooled. Left: the glass is warming up on the surface but the centre part is still cool. Right: during cooling the glass has already cooled on the surface but the centre is still hot. These differences in temperatures could cause cracks later on so it is necessary to always anneal your pieces while using any heat processes.

Annealing is a method of preventing cracks from happening. Glass is held on a specific temperature (heat-soaked) for longer to let the glass heat up evenly. This temperature level is when the glass slowly moves from its solid state to liquid and back. Annealing needs to be done twice during the firing period – once when the glass is heating and once while cooling. This temperature is different for every type of glass and this information should always be provided by the manufacturer.

It may be tricky to know the annealing temperature while working with found glass of unknown origin. In this case you would need to do some tests before making your final piece.

Firing Schedules

Firing glass is not a straightforward process. You are actually forcing the glass to completely change its shape by applying heat. There are usually eight phases in each firing schedule. The firing schedule will be different depending on what kind of project you are doing, the type of glass and the size or type of kiln. You will learn to adjust firing schedules by experience but there are some general rules which will help you to understand the process.

As we said, glass firings require eight phases.

1. **Initial heat:** in this part of firing process the temperature is rising slowly to annealing point. This will allow the glass to heat evenly and prevent it from shattering due to thermal shock. The smaller the pieces of glass, the quicker this stage could be. However, there is no harm in keeping it longer, especially if you are casting.
2. **Anneal soak:** this phase is sometimes called heat soak to distinguish it from the second anneal phase. The temperature is held on the annealing point to allow everything to heat evenly before the next step.
3. **Rapid heat:** this phase could be quite quick as glass is not sensitive to cracking or thermal shock when the temperature

rises above the annealing point. The kiln needs to quickly generate as much heat as possible for this stage to avoid the danger of devitrification – a crystal growth on the surface of the glass which would make the glass appear opaque.

4. **Process soak:** the temperature is held (soaked) at the highest temperature. At this point the glass is liquid and needs some time to do its job, whether it is filling the mould, slumping or fusing.
5. **Rapid cool:** once the right form has been made the temperature needs to drop quickly to keep the shape created. The temperature should not drop below the annealing point.
6. **Anneal soak:** the glass is now returning from liquid to solid form. The whole mass needs to be allowed to go to the same temperature to release any potential stress.
7. **Anneal cool:** the temperature needs to drop very slowly within its annealing range at this phase to relieve as much stress as possible.
8. **Cool to room temperature:** this phase could be little bit faster as all stress should been removed during the previous phases and the glass is already solid and not within its critical range.

It is very important to keep a good record of all your firing schedules. You will probably start with the firing schedules recommended by the manufacturer but as you become more experienced you will be able to adjust the firing schedules depending on the project.

Devitrification

As we learned in Chapter 1, glass is an amorphous material without any crystalline structure. This creates some of its unique properties, such as transparency. Devitrification is a crystal growth on the surface which causes glass to lose that glossiness and to become opaque. This growth may appear when the temperature or the timings of your schedule is not right. It could also be caused by contamination of

Devitrification – a mild example. Clear float glass has become opaque by improper firing temperature. This effect could be used intentionally, as it is in this case: the devitrified part creates a more gentle, translucent layer which fits nicely with silver dust inclusions.

the kiln by dirt or by any inclusions in or on the glass. It is usually an unwanted event but can also be used intentionally in a controlled manner.

Techniques

Fusing and Slumping

Fusing is probably the first kiln forming technique you try. It is relatively easy and you can achieve very beautiful and varied results. It is a very old technique, known since ancient Egyptian times. Fusing basically means heating two or more pieces of glass until they stick (fuse) together. Most often it is flat sheet glass that is used for this technique.

Fusing occurs in stages: slumping, tack fuse and full fuse. Each stage offers different design possibilities. When your piece reaches slumping temperature it becomes soft enough to change its shape and 'slump' over or inside your mould. Tack fuse is useful if you want your pieces of glass to stick together but to more or less keep their shape. The glass will have slightly rounded

edges but the main shape stays the same. If you start increasing the temperature, the layers of the glass start to melt into each other a bit more. During full fuse, the glass layers merge and melt together completely and the piece takes a more uniform shape.

It is important to understand that during fusing the surface of the glass behaves differently from the inside mass. If the glass is not restricted, it will naturally form round edges and soft shapes: it will not form sharp edges unless it is forced to do so by a mould. The degree of roundness depends on the temperature.

Tack Fuse

The highest temperature for tack fuse is about 720–760°C. This depends on the type of glass, the kiln and how long the glass stays at the desired temperature. This information will be provided by the glass manufacturer. If you are working with found glass you need to experiment to find the right temperature.

During tack fusing the glass layers stick together and make a permanent bond but the shape does not change that much. The edges only round a little but the original shape is still visible. This is very useful if you want to keep the glass layers raised.

Fusing can appear in several stages. Left: the piece is tack fused – the edges of the glass stay relatively intact but the layers are stuck together. Centre: the piece is fused at medium temperature – the edges of the piece are starting to round but the layers of glasses still appear distinct. Right: the piece is fully fused – the layers of glass are completely melted together and create one uniform piece.

Full Fuse

The fusing temperature is usually in the range 750–800°C. Again, this temperature depends on the type of glass, so check this information with your glass manufacturer.

At this temperature, pieces are completely fused together and the edges are rounded off. The form changes significantly. When the temperature reaches full fuse temperature, the glass becomes soft and liquid like honey. The skin of the glass collapses and the glass mass starts to move, taking the form of the surface on which it is fused. Here you need to be careful as the glass will stick to anything so using some form of separator is necessary.

6mm Rule

This rule can help you to predict the design outcomes of your pieces to a certain degree. It is based on the fact that, at this stage, if glass is left unrestricted by moulds or any other forces it will have tend to either shrink or spread by 6mm in thickness.

So, for example, if you use just one layer of 3mm glass, it will shrink to make a round shape. If you use two 3mm sheets, one on the top of the other, the size of the fired pieces would stay more or less the same, only the edges will round. If you use, say, three 3mm layers stacked up, the fired piece will fuse into approximately 6mm thickness and spill out sideways.

For example, if you want to make your piece thin but to a certain size, then you have to cut

Sketch to explain the 6mm rule. The pieces on the bottom row are in their raw state; the ones on the top show what happens to the glass after fusing.

the glass much larger as it will shrink. Again, it would be advisable to do some tests before you start with final pieces to understand the behaviour of the glass.

Fire Polishing

Fire polishing is used when you need to re-gloss your piece of glass; for example, after you have ground the edges so they have become matt or when you decide that you want your sandblasted piece to be shiny again. In these cases you don't want your piece to change its shape so that is why fire polishing is usually done at a lower temperature than fusing. Again, the temperature depends on the type of glass used.

Don't forget that your piece needs to go through the annealing stages during fire polishing in the same way as when fusing.

Preparation

It is important that everything inside the kiln is clean. Prepare your kiln with a new layer of shelf primer or kiln paper. Then clean your glass, remove any impurities, dirt or fingerprints: all these can influence the result, as such impurities could fire permanently onto your piece or prevent it from properly joining together where wanted.

Temporary Fixing

There is a useful trick when you are struggling to keep several layers of glass in the right position before fusing. It is possible to use a small amount of organic glue (gum arabic or wallpaper paste) to hold the glass until the fusing occurs. If you use just the minimal amount of glue, it will be burned away without leaving a trace: this is important as you don't want your piece to be ruined by fumes in the kiln.

Multiple Fusing

It is useful to know that glass can be fused more than once. You can cut your already fused glass and rearrange the design. You can also combine

For this piece I wanted to fuse silver chain between several layers of sheet glass. The chain needed to be positioned precisely and it was tricky to balance all the items in the right position. Here, it helped to use a little organic glue to keep all the pieces in the right places until the fusing took place.

different techniques like fusing and slumping. You can use painting, gold leaf or enamels on your fused pieces or work with inclusions. Here again, always remember to use only compatible glasses when combining different techniques.

Slumping

This process involves shaping the glass by using various props and moulds. When heated, the glass becomes soft and takes the form of the surface on which it is placed. If the surface is not flat, gravity will pull the softened glass down to the lowest point available. This means you can use it to form three-dimensional forms like bowls, concave or convex shapes, patterned surfaces and so on. The temperature for slumping is usually lower than that for fusing; check your glass manufacturer's advice for exact firing schedules.

The easiest way is to use some sort of mould and let the glass slump over it. The mould could be made of any material which can withstand the slumping temperature, such as plaster, ceramic-fibre paper, or non-glazed ceramic or metal dishes (preferably stainless steel if the latter). The mould needs to be covered thoroughly by a separator layer to prevent glass sticking to it. Small metal bowls painted with separator can be used to create concave dish shapes: the glass can be bent over the outside or round the inside of the mould.

Another very easy method involves using kiln papers, which come in different thicknesses and shapes. By cutting and arranging pieces of ceramic paper you can achieve different relief and raised areas on your glass pieces. Remember to use mask and gloves when using ceramic fibre as it is an irritant material. Another easy way of creating pattern on your piece is to carve a plaster block and then place your piece of glass onto the carved relief to slump over it.

The first picture shows how the slumping over the mould look like; the second one shows slumping in the mould. When the glass becomes soft it will lie over or fill in any shape below. The easiest way to start is to use some sort of rounded shape like a bowl as glass doesn't form sharp corners easily. Once you get more experience, you may want to try more complex shapes.

A rewarding and easy way of using slumping technique is to cut some shapes from thicker kiln paper and lay them underneath your sheet of glass. Once the glass becomes soft it will slump over those shapes and your final piece will have an interesting texture. You may want to use several layers of kiln paper cut-outs. This technique is especially effective for using with transparent glass as you can see the imprints from both sides.

If you use moulds for your slumping, the bottom part of your piece will take the form of the mould and became matt and the top exposed to the air will be fire polished. If you want your piece to be shiny (fire polished) on both sides, then you can try to slump your piece within the mould without full contact. There would have to be some support of the glass at the sides but the glass will form itself by the force of gravity without the need to touch the mould. With this technique the range of design possibilities is limited to a round shape.

If you practise fusing and slumping for some time you may want to progress into more advanced methods such as combing which creates marble-like effects. What you can produce with these techniques is limitless so let your curiosity to lead you further.

Casting

Casting is a process similar to glass fusing but during the casting process the glass is heated to a higher temperature. The glass then becomes liquid (not just soft and sticky as with fusing temperatures) and can take virtually any form so it is necessary to use a mould which is the negative of your desired shape. For casting purposes we use 'refractory' moulds, the term indicating that for making the mould we use a material which is resistant to heat and will survive the firing temperature inside the kiln. Traditionally, a mixture of plaster and silica is used for this process. In order to be able to make a mould you need some kind of master shape to start with.

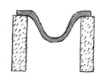

This is another, slightly more advanced slumping technique. You place your sheet glass on top of some kiln furniture elements or props and let the glass slump in mid-air without any mould. You need to be very precise with the timing here, otherwise the glass will slump too much. The best option is if you can visually check the progress of the slumping.

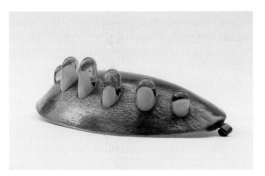 

Nicki Lawrence's *Sea Slug* brooch shows an interesting, experimental use of the slumping technique. She is using a copper brooch shape with the holes filled by glass. When the whole piece is heated, the glass starts to pour through the holes. Here is her detailed explanation of the process: 'The blue nudibranch (sea slug) brooch was made from sheet copper which I drilled then domed on a hydraulic press. The domed copper, layered with pieces of reactive bullseye glass, was then fired, allowing the glass to flow through the holes, forming the tentacles. Tabs, to attach the brooch pin, were left as the final piece was cut, filed and finished, using liver of sulphur to blacken it.' (Photo: Rudi Peeling)

Mould Making

You can either buy the glass casting plaster mix already prepared or you can make your own. The simple but effective recipe is to use one part of plaster to one part of silica mixture. Silica is added to the plaster to make the mould stronger and help it to resist the heat. There are hundreds of different recipes for refractory mould mixtures for different purposes which you can check online. Each serious glass caster seems to have their own. I have had good results from casting small glass objects in moulds made of investment plaster normally used for metal casting: the composition is very similar and the mould easily withstands the temperature. But when starting, I would recommend the basic mixture specified above.

There are two ways of making moulds, depending on the shape of your master model. It is simple to make an open mould if your master model has no undercuts and can easily be taken out of the mould before firing. In this case the master could be made from any material – clay, wax, plastic, metal, wood, rubber. Your casting would be a relief, taking the shape of the inside of your mould with a flat back where the mould is open.

If you want to keep the full three-dimensional shape of your model then you need to use a

different method called lost wax casting. It follows similar principles to the jewellery castings you may be familiar with. Your master model will need to be made out of wax.

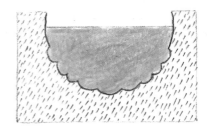

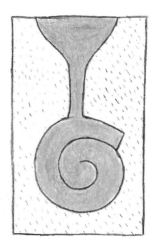

Open and closed moulds. The open mould is much simpler but is suitable only for items with no undercuts and the result would always have a flat back. More complex shapes need to be cast in closed moulds.

First, we will look at how to make your master model and then we progress into mould making and finally filling the mould with the raw glass material.

Making a Wax Master Model: Traditional and Digital Methods

You may choose to carve or sculpt your master directly in wax. This would be the easiest way but you would be able to use the shape only once as it will disappear in the process (hence the name 'lost' wax casting). There are specialist waxes for glass casting which are designed for this process but you may choose to experiment with other kinds.

If you have previously carved wax for metal castings then don't expect the glass to be able to reproduce such fine detail as metal. The glass naturally rounds itself when heated unless it is forced into a different shape. Have you ever watched the water spilled on a flat surface? The water has a tendency to form rounded edges and any droplets repeat this on a smaller scale. Glass has a similar behaviour: it doesn't like to form sharp edges when heated. There are some techniques which help to overcome this, as we will discuss later.

Multiplying Masters

If you want to have multiple waxes of your master or your master is made out of clay, metal or any other material, you will have to make a mould out of it. This time the mould needs to be made out of flexible material which allows you to take out your models. You can use a cold silicon mould, which is suitable for a master shape made of any material, or a rubber mould, which is suitable for materials which can withstand the heat of liquid rubber being poured over them (clay, metal, wood, some plastics). There is a very useful rubber material called Gelflex which is easy to melt and can be recycled several times.

Another option is to make a digital file of your desired shape and have it 3D printed directly in wax or resin (the latter being the cheaper option). The 3D modelling programs allow you to design shapes you may not be able to model by hand and you can experiment with different designs virtually before committing your time and resources to making the actual object.

You need to make a silicon or rubber mould out of your printed resin master to be able to make multiple of waxes for casting as described above. 3D printing technology is becoming easily accessible with the basic home printers sold by some electronic retailers. Alternatively, you can send your file to be printed by a specialist company.

There are some experiments being done with using 3D printing technology to print directly in glass but this is not widely available at the time of writing this book.

Making a Refractory Mould

First, you need to make some sort of base which will encapsulate your model and hold the liquid refractory mix until it hardens. For this you can use clay, a piece of plastic or some similar waterproof material which will not stick to plaster. If you

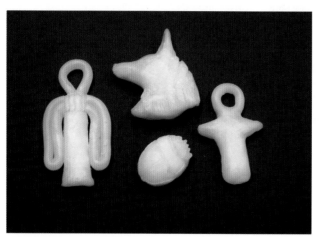

Wax masters inspired by ancient Egyptian amulets and made from casting wax.

are making an open mould it would be enough to place your wax model directly on the bottom of the mould with a small extra raised platform made out of clay or other material. Secure the model to the surface with its flat side facing down. Make sure your piece is placed in the middle and there is enough space around it.

If you are using a 3D shape the mould making is slightly more complex. You need to secure the model on the bottom of the mould on a raised conical or round shape to create an empty space in the finished mould which will later hold the glass and help it to flow easily into your mould.

Make sure the sides of your mould are suffi- ciently high and wide to enclose your model fully. It is also important to check that there is plenty of space between the sides of your mould and your model; you wouldn't want your glass spilled all over the kiln because your mould wasn't strong enough. The next step is to prepare the refractory mix with which to fill your mould.

For this you can either use a casting mixture bought from a specialist (then you would follow the manufacturer's advice on the ratio of material and water) or you can make your own from one part water, one part silica and one part plaster. Always put the mix into the water, never the other way round. Make sure you mix the ingredients evenly so there are no chunks but not too violently as you don't want air bubbles entering the mixture. A few taps on the side of the container or onto a hard surface

In this pendant Angela Thwaites used a digitally designed and printed master for her cast piece. First she makes a CAD model, then a 3D print in PLA or castable resin and then makes a refractory investment mould around the print. The sacrificial stage is when the refractory mould is fired in a kiln to melt out the resin or burn out the print, leaving a clean cavity into which to cast the glass. (Photo: Dave Lawson)

are usually enough to get big bubbles to the surface.

Pour your refractory mix carefully into your mould and let it set for a few hours. Then you can take your mould out and very carefully remove the master (in the case of an open mould). If you are using closed moulds you need to steam the wax out the mould as you won't have access inside. For this you can use a wallpaper steaming machine or similar device

The easy way of making a mould is to place your master wax on a raised platform on a layer of clay. You can then use a piece of thin flexible plastic as the sides of your mould. The clay is soft and mouldable, easy to remove once the plaster mould is finished.

Pouring the refractory mix made of plaster and silica mixed with water in the 1:1:1 ratio.

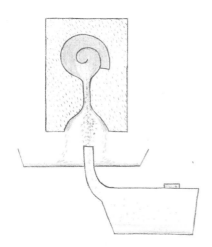

When you are making closed moulds you need to steam the wax master out of the flask: use a wallpaper steamer with the steam outlet placed close to the entrance of the mould. The dripping wax can be caught in the tray filled with water and reused. Make sure you steam out all the wax from the mould as any residue will interfere with the casting process later.

with its outlet placed close to the entrance of your mould. The mould needs to be placed upside down with some space under it to let the wax run away. It is difficult to see inside the mould but you can visually check the entrance of the mould and if you don't see any traces of the wax, the mould should be empty. Then let the mould dry out ready for casting.

The diagrams opposite summarize the process described for making and using a closed mould for lost wax casting.

Filling a Mould

Filling the mould can be a bit tricky. Unfortunately, molten glass does not behave the same way as water and doesn't necessarily fill the mould evenly. As we said before, the glass has a tendency to shrink into itself and create rounded edges. It is relatively easy to fill open moulds by just placing glass inside the mould. In the case of a closed mould you place the material in the reservoir (empty space) above the mould. Alternatively, you can use, say, a terracotta flower pot with the hole in the middle placed directly

above your mould. The glass will then be stored in the pot and poured down the pot's hole into your mould during the casting.

I can't really advise you on a definite strategy here as every mould will be different but generally the material needs to be strategically placed into every part of the mould. This would apply especially to an open mould. You need to be particularly careful with small thin spaces. In general, using slightly more material is better than less. It is easier to grind the excess material off your work than deal with half-cast shapes.

Sometimes it is difficult to judge how much material to use to fill the moulds. You can use a simple technique by using water: a jug is an ideal container. Mark the initial level without

To make a closed mould, first make a wax master model exactly the size of your desired glass piece. Don't forget to make a little platform which will later reverse to provide a reservoir for the raw glass material when starting to cast.

Make a plaster mould around the model.

Steam the wax completely out of the mould.

Once the mould is dry, fill it with the raw glass and place it in the kiln.

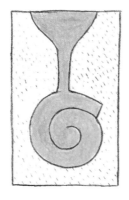

After casting you need to wait until the mould cools down to room temperature.

Break the mould and release your cast; breaking the mould should be easy as it softens during the firing.

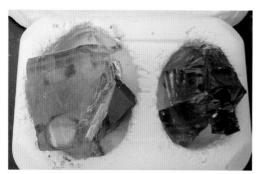

Filling the mould requires experimentation; here, I am using big chunks of transparent glass in different shades of blue.

the glass inside, then submerge your master in the jug until it is covered with water and mark the raised water level. Take the master out and start adding raw glass material until the water reaches the raised mark again.

This technique is suitable for larger chunks of glass, not really for frits or powders. While using these, you would have to judge the quantity by eye. Remember that there is always a lot of air in between the grains so you need to add a little more material.

You will get different results by using different raw materials. If you want your piece to remain transparent it is better to use larger pieces of glass. If you are using small crushed pieces of transparent glass, your cast piece will become translucent to opaque as there will be many tiny air bubbles trapped inside the mass and causing this effect. You can use this effect intentionally when you want to create a 'ghosted' effect. In that case you combine large pieces of transparent glass with finely crushed glass (which

could be coloured or not). The crushed glass will create the opaque layers inside the transparent glass.

Mixing different colours of glass is possible but the results would be slightly unpredictable. The exception is the pâte de verre technique which allows you to position your colours very precisely in specified spaces.

Casting Firing Schedule

The firing temperature for the glass casting would again vary depending on the type of glass you are using and on the size of your piece. Generally, the casting temperature for casting is higher than the one for fusing. You want your glass to become fully liquid, rather than just sticky as it does when fusing. The glass needs to be held on the highest point for a while so that it has some time to spread evenly in your mould. Also, the final annealing and cooling speed should be slower than with fusing. The basic rule is the bigger your piece, the slower your firing should be. If, one day, you decide to do a monumental cast piece of glass then it may take several months or even years for the piece to cool down safely. In the jewellery scale a few hours will be sufficient. For exact firing temperatures for your type of glass check your supplier's advice.

Pâte de verre

This technique has an interesting history; it was actually one of the first glass techniques used in the ancient world. One of the earliest recipes was found in ancient Mesopotamia written on clay tablets and can be dated to between the fourteenth and twelfth centuries BCE.[4] With the development of blowing techniques by the Romans it lost its popularity and was nearly forgotten but returned in the nineteenth century, emerging at the famous Sèvres artist

The easiest way of measuring the material needed for your cast; this method is suitable for most pieces.

training centre in France. Another revival of this technique happened after the Second World War with the rise of the Studio Craft Movement.

The term 'pâte de verre' is French, meaning 'glass paste'. And that pretty much describes the material used. Instead of using solid pieces of glass this technique uses ground glass mixed with a binding material to create a shape. Different effects can be achieved with roughly or finely ground glass. The crushed grains of glass are used to fill a mould by pressing the mixture against the walls of the mould. In this way you can create a hollow shape and that is why the binder is added to the glass mixture to help the glass hold that shape. The mould with the glass is then heated until the grains fuse together and the binder is burnt off. This technique is especially interesting for jewellers as it allows you to create hollow shapes and thus reduce the weight of your piece. This means that you can create larger and lighter pieces than when using solid glass.

Another advantage of this technique is that you can control the colours much more than you can in casting, for example. This technique basically works like sculpting with different coloured glasses, although you build your shape in the opposite way to traditional sculpting techniques, since you fill the mould with colours for the top layer first, working backwards and pressing the successive layers against the walls of your mould.

The process of making is similar to that of casting. You make a refractory mould which you fill with the glass frit. The frit needs to be mixed with water and an organic binder, such

Mariliin Laas uses recycled bottle glass to create her pieces. She chooses to fire at lower temperatures to keep the granular effect of the fused frits. The rough texture here contrasts satisfyingly with the smooth metal setting. (Photo: Valdek Laur)

as gum arabic, to keep its shape. The process of filling the mould is similar that of wetpacking enamels although methods vary: some people fill the damp mould with the glass mixture, others recommend drying the mould before firing. For a small-scale piece all of them will work so you can try each and see what works for you. The pictures here show an example of small-scale mould making for this process.

For small-scale casting, I like to use a standard plastic container that is easily available. Here, I am going to make a mould from a shell. I attach the shell to the bottom of the container with plasticine (or you can use pottery clay). There shouldn't be any undercut in your setting which would prevent the model from being lifted from the mould later on. You may want to paint the shell with some mould release solution to make the lifting the model from the mould easier later on.

Pour your refractory mix over and leave it to dry.

Once the mould is solid, take the plaster out of the plastic container. Peel the plasticine and carefully lift the shell out from your mould, making sure you do not damage the latter.

Fill the mould with frit glass mixed with a little bit of organic binder such as gum arabic, pressing the mixture against the walls of the mould. The binder will help the glass stay in its position before it fuses together.

Use different coloured frits or mix the frits with metal oxides to make your own colours.

Michelle Stewart's series of brooches *What Have You Got to Lose?* are made by the technique of pâte de verre with recycled glass. She explain the idea behind her choice of material: 'I am using recycled glass that has been collected from the site-specific area of the Central Victorian Highlands – the focus of the plant species too. I have collected the glass from within the National and State

Parks and from along roadsides. Then I process it to powder for the pâte de verre. The plant species is an Australian tree fern, one of the first plants to rejuvenate after fire, which is also significant for this area. We have just commemorated the ten-year anniversary of the devastating Black Saturday bush fires.' (Photo: Andrew Barcham)

Different results of different temperatures. If you want to keep a grainy, crumbling appearance for your pieces which is still strong then choose a lower fusing temperature. The grains of the frit fuse together but the individual grains stay visible. If you would like a smoother shape then choose a higher casting temperature for your firings.

You can buy different coloured frit; there is a wide selection available from glass suppliers. Or you may want to make your own by crushing glass into small pieces. You can also experiment with adding different metal oxides to clear frit to add colour.

Choose the firing schedule for pâte de verre according to what you want to create. If you choose a lower temperature the frit grains will fuse together but the individual grains will stay visible. If you increase the temperature the frit grains will melt completely and create a smooth casting. You can make a comparison from the illustration here. For exact temperatures please check the manufacturer's recommended firing temperature for your frit as this will differ depending on your choice.

Recycling Found Glass

For most of the kiln formed techniques is possible to use some sort of recycled glass. For example, you can use found float (window) glass for your fusing or casting projects or small glass beads and glass crystals for decorating your designs. Both the artists whose work has been shown in the last group of illustrations are using recycled found glass ground for pâte de verre techniques.

Using found glass is cheap and possibly more environment-friendly but there are several challenges to consider while using found glass in kiln formed processes. They all have a solution so please don't be put off from using found glass in your projects. First, these glasses are not formulated for use in kiln formed processes. There is a much higher risk of devitrification

and other things that could go wrong quite easily so you need to be more careful. Secondly, there is no advice on firing temperatures and therefore no recommended annealing point, so using found glass will require you to make some experiments before you work out the right temperatures. Each found glass will be different so you need to repeat this process for every new found item. Lastly, it is very likely that this glass will not be compatible with any other glasses you are using. You will have to make compatibility tests for each type of glass or just stick to using one kind of glass for each project.

Another example of Michelle Stewart's *Fossil Brooches* made from site-specific found glass: 'The fossil brooches feature a rare plant that has re-emerged in the past ten years and is endemic only to the area of the Central Victorian Highlands. This is a particularly important area of forest and holds many rare, endangered and critically endangered species – both plants and animals – and is being clear fell-logged, which devastates the whole area.' (Photo: Andrew Barcham)

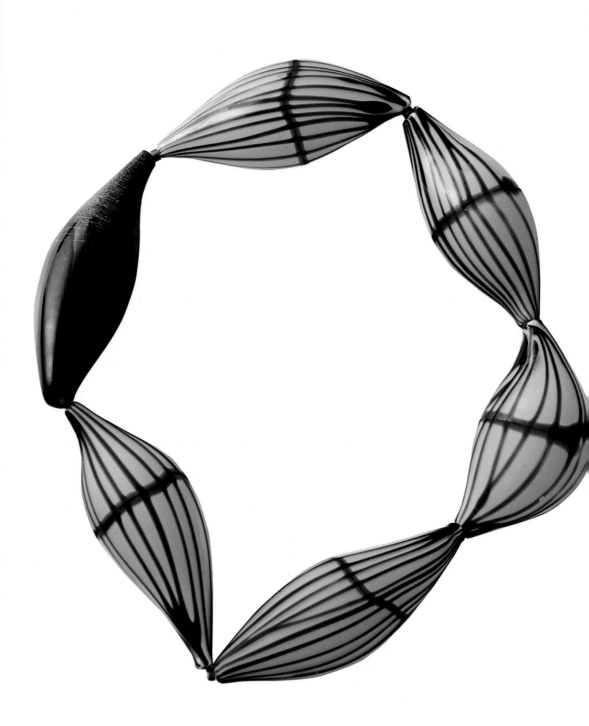

HEAT PERFORMING TECHNIQUES 2: LAMPWORKING

Lampwork is a fascinating and rewarding way of manipulating glass. It differs from other techniques in that you use an open flame for shaping your pieces, which is why this set of techniques is sometimes known as 'flamework'. It is the most direct heat forming technique introduced in this book as hot glass is shaped by using the movement of the hands over the flame. Using this technique will give you an understanding of how glass behaves in its liquid state, which will then inform your kiln forming practice.

As the name suggests, in lampworking you are using a lamp or torch to melt the glass.

LEFT: **Catarina Zucchi is an Italian lampworker reinventing the thousand-year-old history of Murano glass jewellery and using blown glass elements for her pieces. She talks about her inspiration and materials used: 'It's the game between light and opacity, between shade and colour. The sinuous shapes of blown glass create an elegant and sophisticated composition. The black colour element, scratched on one side, breaks the composition by contrasting the chromatic sequence. The elements, one close to the other, create a rich and elegant accessory, their surface, finely sandblasted for half, enhances the volume of the elements. Black lines hide or conceal green lines? Is the sandblasted surface opaque or brightens half the glass bead?** *The Light and Shadow* **necklace is an experience to wear.' (Photo: Chiara and Francesca Nicolosi)**

For this, thin rods or strips of glass are melted directly in the flame. When glass is in its malleable state its shape is defined by different hand movements and by the various tools. Small-scale blowing techniques can be used in lampwork as well, which makes it similar to larger-scale hot-blown glass.

It is primarily known as a bead-making technique but its use is much wider. You will probably start with making beads and there is a lot to learn but later on you may want to progress to much more sculptural pieces like small vessels, flowers or small-scale sculptures. One of the best examples of how precise and varied lampworking can be is the collection of underwater fauna and flora models by German masters Eduard and Rudolf Blatschka from the nineteenth century. But, of course, there are many contemporary artists who have mastered this technique and I will introduce some of them later.

Materials and Tools

For lampworking, you need a different set of equipment from any other kind of glass making we have discussed so far. The glass you use comes in long thin rods, usually soda-lime or borosilicate glass. In the past, lead glass was used as it allowed a wide scale of colours but on the other hand it is quite heavy. For melting the

You can use lampworking techniques to create all sorts of shapes. Özge Erbilen Yalçin's brooch from her *Nightingale's Eye* collection has been inspired by traditional Ottoman glass art; she uses the spiral surface patterns known as 'nightingale's eye' in this beautifully executed brooch. She aspires to produce contemporary pieces but also to establish a multifaceted and rich connection with the past. (Photo: Tolga Özdemir)

glass you need a lamp or torch strong enough to melt the glass. And for shaping your glass you need various tools as you cannot touch the hot glass directly with your hands.

Glass for Lampworking

There are two kind of glass used for lampworking: soft and hard. Soft glass can be either soda-lime or lead glass manufactured in rods about 5–8mm thick. It is produced by many glass manufacturers so the range of colours and glasses with special effects is very wide. This glass is easy to melt at lower temperatures and can be used with any kind of torch. It makes a perfect glass for beginners. It is very important to check the CEO of each range as each producer has different technical specifications.

A lot of the soft lampworking glass is produced with a CEO of 104, so some ranges could be mixed together but not all of them. It is usually easiest to choose one manufacturer and stick to them to avoid compatibility issues. This applies to decorative glass elements such as stringers, frits and beads: all of them need to be the same CEO as your rods.

Hard glass is borosilicate glass which is what is used in laboratories and for medical glass equipment. It is very hard and durable but requires a more powerful flame to be melted. This glass is workable only with an oxygen-gas torch. There are slightly fewer colour options for this type of rods but there is still enough variety to choose from. The advantage would be as said before – its durability. This could be quite helpful for more exposed jewellery pieces such as bracelets or long pendants. It is also

This is a lampworking station of Czech lampworker Petra Hamplová in her Prague studio. You can see a gas torch with its eye protection, the rod rest placed in front of the torch and a selection of glass rods, stringers and lampworking tools close to hand.

more resistant to thermal shock so you do not need to be quite so careful with leaving the glass outside the flame for a little longer.

There are also some special effect glasses such as dichroic glasses, double helix or aventurine glasses with little crystals of metals inside them. Depending on what you select you can achieve metallic, rainbow or pearl effects and much more. There is a wide variety of these special effect glasses available from glass suppliers.

It is possible to use thinly cut sheet glass instead of round rods but it will require a bit more work from you. This glass will be more difficult to heat and melt evenly so you need to spend more time on it. Because of this, it may be more susceptible to thermal shock.

The Lamp or Torch

There is a variety of torches available but basically they differ by the fuel used. As a beginner you may start with the more simple gas torch; to use this you just need to attach the torch to the gas canister. A lampworking torch is very similar to a jeweller's torch, only the flame needs to be strong enough to melt the glass. Also, it needs to be secured safely to your working place as you will need both hands free for manipulating the glass and mandrels.

The gas torch runs entirely on gas and is reasonably affordable. This may be your first purchase if you want to try this technique without committing yourself to buying expensive equipment.

Another variant is the oxygen-propane torch. This looks similar but needs two kinds of fuel – gas and oxygen. It is quieter and stronger but powerful enough to melt even borosilicate glass. The set-up is more complicated as you will need both an oxygen concentrator and a gas canister feeding your flame. These would be a more significant expense but the torch is definitely a more versatile tool.

Cooling Substances

A cooling substance is needed to slow down the cooling process and thus prevent the thermal shock which could cause cracks in your lamp-work. This could be either ceramic fibre blankets or some kind of mineral material which consists of a large proportion of air. Finely ground vermiculite in a large pot is a good option; you can

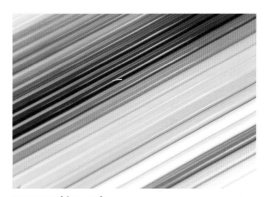
Lampworking rods.

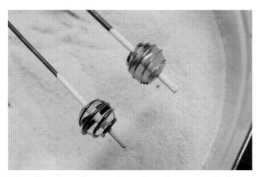
Metallic glass decoration placed on top of glass beads.

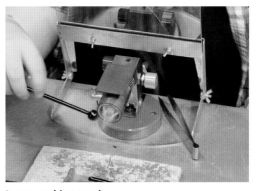
Lampworking torch.

Pot with cooling mixture; here I am using vermiculite grains purchased from a local gardening centre.

buy this from your glass supplier or in a DIY/ gardening store.

Later on, when you want to make more complex pieces, it would be advisable to invest in an annealing kiln. The finished lampwork is put directly into the kiln to even out the surface and inside temperatures of your glass and then allowed to cool down very slowly. This is the safest way to protect your beads or other work from cracking.

Tools

Molten glass behaves like a rather thick honey. It flows slowly so you can manipulate it by using gravity, rotating your work in different directions, or by using tools. Remember to use the tools cold, outside the flame if possible and only for a short while, otherwise they may stick to the glass permanently. If this happens, you can stay away from the flame for a minute, then wiggle the tool out or submerge the tool in cold water so that the glass falls out. Metal cools down more quickly than glass so these techniques are usually successful. A last resort would be to break the glass carefully.

Mandrel and Bead Separator
These are tools used for bead making and they are basically straight metal wires of different thicknesses and about 20–30cm long. The thickness of the wire will determine the size of the bead. The best to use is stainless steel as it doesn't conduct the heat as quickly as, say,

copper. The top (working) part of the mandrel needs to be covered by a separator, otherwise the glass can stick to the metal permanently. This is usually done by dipping the mandrel into some sort of clay-based substance such as kaolin mixed with water.

Marver
This is a flat heatproof surface which is used to flatten, rotate or otherwise shape your beads. It can be made of any heatproof material, the most common being metals such as stainless steel or marble or graphite. Some torches have a marver already built in close to the flame outlet, which is quite handy. But you may improvise and use your jewellery steel hammering block for this purpose.

It is important to remember that while you are using marver (or any other tool) you are cooling down the area of the glass which is in contact with the tool. The glass mass contracts and creates a characteristic 'fingerprint' pattern on the surface while the rest of the bead still has a fluid, honey-like consistency. This causes stress within your bead which can later create a crack or shatter the bead. You need to put your bead in the flame and even out the temperatures.

Other Equipment
For manipulating hot glass in the flame you can either use gravity, shaping the glass by holding the work this way or that, or you can use various tools. There are useful specialist glass shaping tools you can buy such as forming tools for round beads or pattern-making tweezers. But you can also use a lot of tools you may already have in your workshop or household. The only

A rod rest is a helpful tool. This is a traditional one but if you are just starting out it is possible to use something simple, such as a sheet of metal folded in half with holes for placing the rods.

rule is that the tools are made from some sort of heat-resistant material such as metal, graphite and so on. You can use metal tools for shaping, pinching, imprinting or scribing. Steel tweezers are probably the essential tool for shaping, pinching and removing excess material and dirt from your piece. Metal scissors are useful for cutting thin layers of glass: the best are the ones with long thin blades. I personally like using an old steel fork, knife and spoon for shaping my pieces: the fork is useful for indenting, the knife for shaping flat surfaces and fixing unevenness, and the spoon for shaping concave and convex surfaces. You can also use some of your jewellery tools, such as the bottom part of your doming tool for cabochon shaping.

Rod Rest

When you start working with your glass rods you will realize that the top of your rod stays hot for a while after you stop working with it. You need some sort of rod rest so you can securely place your rods without burning your working surface. It could be a simple home-made metal stand with round grooves on the end or you may look for a traditional cast steel lampworking rest. Such a rest has the advantage that if

Lampworked rings by Charlotte Verity. 'I blow individual miniature hollow components; spherical bubbles or straight drops, often from bullseye coloured glass rods and Schott colourless glass tube. I often fill the transparent bubbles or drops with tiny, round, faceted laboratory-grown stones. The stones are created under intense heat and can therefore withstand the conditions as the glass component is returned to the flame or kiln for the subsequent process. Working with transparent glass allows for the transmission of light; an aesthetic quality that enables objects behind the glass to remain visible, though sometimes distorted or magnified.' (Photo: Charlotte Verity)

placed underneath your flame, it can keep your rods warm and thus makes them easier to use again.

Working Surface

The basic requirement of your working surface is that it is made from some sort of heatproof material. You may use heatproof old tiles or a steel desktop to cover your table. Remove any material which is flammable from your working environment, especially anything in front of your flame. You may get some hot pieces of glass flying around so you need to be careful: this is more likely to happen at the beginning before you learn how glass behaves in the flame.

Health and Safety

I hope these safety rules don't scare you and prevent you from enjoying lampwork. They are important, as you are working with an open flame and flammable gas. They are all common sense but it is always good to repeat the basics.

Eye Goggles

Always wear eye protection while working with glass. There are two main reasons. First, you must protect your eyes from the tiny pieces of glass that may fly around when you heat your piece too quickly. Some lampworkers use a transparent screen in front of their torches for the same reason. The second reason is that some people may be sensitive to the light glow which molten glass emits. Staring at the flame for extended periods of time may make your eyes tired. This light emission is much stronger if you are using oxygen-propane fuel, in which case I would strongly recommend you invest in special protective goggles which block this particular kind of light but leave your vision intact. That way you can see what you are doing and be safe at the same time. You can purchase these from specialist suppliers.

Working with a Open Flame

Remember that you are working with a naked flame so be very careful to remove any flammable objects from the direction of the flame and around your working space. Have your tools and glass rods ready on the appropriate sides of your working surface as it is difficult to swap tools to the other hand during the work.

If you have long hair it should be tied back. Do not wear any loose scarves or anything which could accidentally catch fire when you are working. It is recommended that you wear long-sleeved clothes made from natural fibres while working as they are less flammable. Also, choose sensible shoes, preferably not sandals or any other open footwear, to prevent any burns.

Never leave the lit torch unattended. Also, make sure that small children or animals cannot access your work area.

Hot Items

Remember that the glass, your tools, the working surface and the torch stay hot long after you finish the work. The fact that they are not glowing red any more doesn't mean they are cool enough to touch. Always allow sufficient time for cooling before you touch anything with bare hands and always use heat-protective gloves when unsure.

Ventilation

Ideally, you should have an exhaust fan but an open window will be enough at the start. This is really essential as most fuels do not burn 100 per cent: a small amount of gas will stay in the air and give off carbon monoxide. This is a transparent, odourless gas which is hazardous for humans or any living animals. It is especially dangerous for ill people, smokers and pregnant women. The characteristic unpleasant smell of gas is not carbon monoxide but an additive which is mixed into gas fuels to warn you of any leakage. If you start to feel dizzy or nauseous, stop immediately and get some fresh air. It is a good idea to have a gas detector in your studio.

Before You Start Making

Preparing the Mandrels

In case you are making beads, you need to prepare your mandrels by dipping them in the release agent – usually some sort of clay-based substance – needed to prevent the molten glass from sticking onto your metal wire. You can buy the mixture already made or make your own from fine-ground kaolin sand and water (distilled water is better); the mixture should have a yoghurt-like consistency.

I usually clean the mandrels with a kitchen metal scrubbing pad to roughen the surface slightly. Dip the mandrels into the solution: 5–7cm is enough working space for a bead. Then let the solution dry upright for about thirty minutes. The layer should be even, with no bubbles. Uneven surface and other impurities can peel off during the work and damage your bead. It is better to prepare plenty of mandrels in advance so you do not have to stop once you start working with the flame.

Lighting the Torch

Turn on your gas and light your burner. Add oxygen to the flame (if you have this type of torch). Keep adding gas/oxygen until you are happy with the strength of your flame. This may take a bit of practice as each torch will be slightly different so follow the manufacturer's advice.

The common mistake at the beginning is that your heated glass will change colour to an unwanted shade. If you work too close to the

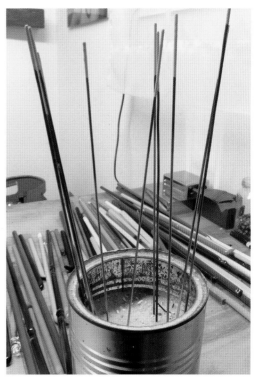

A useful trick for keeping your mandrels straight while they are drying is to have a container filled with sand; it makes it very easy to insert or remove your mandrels.

strongest part of the flame, your glass may turn into greyish, murky colours. It is because that part of the flame you are using is the one which consumes most of the oxygen needed to keep the nice colours of your glass from changing. It usually helps to reduce the strength of the flame or to work higher up.

Next, we will look at how to make a basic bead shape, probably the first thing you attempt to create with this technique before progressing into more complex shapes.

Making a Basic Bead

Start by heating your glass rod slowly. If you insert the rod directly into the hottest part of the

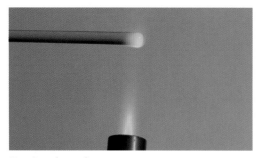

Heating the rod.

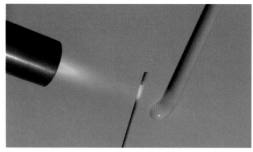

Heating the mandrel.

Winding the molten glass onto the mandrel.

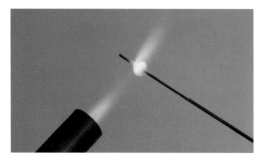

Bead rounding.

Finished bead on mandrel.

Finished bead.

flame, little pieces of the glass could start breaking off your rod. Introduce the rod to the flame slowly by moving the top of the rod in and out of the top (weaker) part of the flame. Gradually leave the rod in the flame longer and longer. Simultaneously, rotate the rod so the material is heated thoroughly. After a while, the colour of the glass will start to change. Do not worry; the colour will return to its original after the glass cools down. At that point you can move the rod to the stronger part of the flame; hold the rod horizontal and keep rotating it. The end of your rod will start to glow with a bright orange light. This means your glass is starting to melt. Keep going until about 1–1.5cm of your rod is melted and a round end has been created. At that point the melted material start to droop downwards so you need to keep rotating your rod.

Once your glass is ready you need to heat your mandrel a bit so the working temperatures of both surfaces are similar. Put the mandrel into a flame for a few seconds and rotate it but keep your glass rod in as well. The rod is ready when you see a red glow. This may require a bit of practice as you need to use both hands at the same time.

Now you are ready to start winding the molten glass around your mandrel. The easiest way is to stick the rod onto the mandrel from the top; hold your glass rod still and rotate the mandrel away from you. This should be done quite lightly; do not try to push the rod by force as you may damage the protective layer on the mandrel. The rod needs to stay in the flame all the time. Once you use all the molten material, pull the rod away. Repeat the process until you have the required number of beads. Rest the rod somewhere safe as the top is still hot.

The first few beads you make will probably be a bit wonky but you can make adjustments to the bead by rotating and moving the mandrel with the melted material. The glass will have a tendency to round itself when heated. If you keep your bead rotating in the flame long enough it will become satisfactorily rounded.

Once you are happy with the shape you need to anneal your bead. If you take your bead from the flame to the room temperature too quickly, the glass will cool down on the surface faster than the inside. This will cause a tension inside your bead which could then create a crack or even shatter the bead. To prevent this from happening you need to move your finished bead to a cooler area of your flame and let it cool down slowly. The bead will start losing its glow and become darker. Once the surface is hardened you can move your bead to the cooling substance, between the ceramic fibre sheets or into an annealing kiln for about twenty minutes to an hour, depending on the size of the bead. Do not check the bead until it has cooled down completely: you risk the bead being cracked by the sudden change of temperature. When you start making bigger or more complicated beads and other lampwork an annealing kiln would be necessary.

Remove the bead from the mandrel. When your beads are completely cooled down, submerge them in a container with water. Water will dissolve the separating layer and you will be able to take the bead off the mandrel. If the bead sticks, you can carefully surround it with a cloth or paper towel and use pliers to twist the mandrel gently; this should be enough to release the bead. If you still have problems, try soaking the beads in water overnight.

If your glass bead accidentally came into contact with the steel rod directly it would stick to the metal permanently. You would need to either carefully crush the glass to release the mandrel or dispose of the whole thing.

Cleaning the Bead

When you remove your bead from the mandrel you will notice that some of the separator is probably still attached inside the hole. To clean this, soak the bead in water and use pipe cleaners or special bead-making scrapers.

You may also find some sharp edges and uneven surfaces on your beads. To remove these use diamond files or pads, or use your pendant drill with a diamond bit. Remember to

These are special tools of varied thicknesses for cleaning the inside of the beads; you could try using pipe cleaners for similar effect.

Red Popcorn Necklace, Petra Hamplová. She is using coral red Czech glass to make her 'popcorn' beads. The individual beads started with simple round beads which have been shaped into more expressive shapes. Strung together they create a continuous playful arrangement. (Photo: Petra Hamplová)

use them wet – you do not want to breathe in glass powder containing silica.

If you need to remove and fix larger areas and you are unhappy with the matt surface, you can always carefully fire polish the whole bead again. Remember that you need to anneal the bead as well.

Shaping the Hot Glass

While working on your beads or other work you can use different ways of shaping and decorating your work. There are many techniques but here we can cover only the basic ones. Once you understand how the glass mass behaves you will be able to combine different methods and start coming up with your own ways of making. For more advanced methods please refer to specialist lampworking publications or online tutorials.

Cylinder Shapes

For making a cylindrical shape, you need to roll a little more molten material onto your mandrel than for a round bead. When the whole piece is heated evenly and is soft, you can then start rolling the bead against the marver. Try not to put too much pressure onto the bead, just

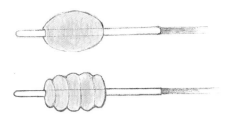

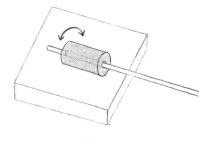

Making cylindrical beads.

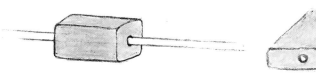

Making cylindrical beads with flat, square and triangular cross-sections.

gently roll the mandrel there and back; the glass mass will be compressed into a cylindrical shape naturally.

Flat, Square or Triangular Shapes

For making any flat shape you press the well-heated glass onto your marver or use some wider flat tool such as a knife blade. Make sure to put your glass back into the flame to even out the temperatures: when you press the glass onto the cold tool, you cool down one side of the bead; this could cause the cracking in the glass later.

Be careful not to heat the glass for too long otherwise you start losing the flat shape. It is safer to work in a cooler part of the flame if you are working for a longer period of time on one bead.

Conical Shapes

Making a conical shape is very similar to making a cylindrical shape but while rolling the glass onto the mandrel back and forth, you hold the mandrel at about a 45-degree angle. That way, the glass mass will naturally make the desired shape. You may want to reheat the bead a few times during the work as you will notice that the glass cools quite quickly.

Pinching, Poking, Forming

You can use your tools in a wide variety of ways to shape your pieces into all kind of wonderful creations. While working with hot glass you will become aware of its movement and possibilities; actual practical experience is essential

Making conical beads.

to gain this understanding. It may be slightly tricky to create precise flat and sharp surfaces but it is very effective with any kind of organic shape. Imagine working with a thick honey which could also freeze if cooled. You can use a variety of tools specially made for lampworking but it is fine to use any metal tools available. I use some of my jewellery or household tools such as tweezers, knifes, scissors or soldering pins for lampworking as well. Make sure you cool down your tool in cold water between each use.

Use a sharp steel tool to make holes and spots. Just make sure you do not pinch all the way to the mandrel: the separator layer may get damaged and your glass will stick to the metal wire permanently.

You can use tweezers to raise the surface of a piece. You can flatten the parts of your work and sculpt various shapes. Make sure you heat your piece enough but not too much – otherwise the glass will start falling into itself and creating a round ball.

Scissors are very useful for creating cone-like textures or snipping the edges of your pieces. Just make sure that you use your scissors quickly so the glass doesn't stick to them.

Marbling

The effect of marbling is easily achieved by manipulating two or more colours with various tools. Experiment to see how different movements create different effects; for example, from a plain dot you can create an eye or a heart shape. Coloured glass looks very effective in combination with layers of transparent glass.

Doming Tools

If you would like to make a perfectly round bead or glass cabochon, there are special-ist lampworking forms available. It is possible to use your jewellery forming tools or stainless steel spoon for the same purpose. In this way you can create your own glass version of precious and semi-precious stones in whatever colour combination you want.

Decorative Lampworking Techniques

We will now look at a few basic ways of embellishing the surface of your work. Once you learn

Marbling effect: another example from Özge Erbilen Yalçin's *Nightingale's Eye* collection. In this brooch, Özge is recreating a traditional Ottoman lampworking technique, manipulating hot blue and white glass with sharp tools to create these swirling patterns. (Photo: Tolga Özdemir)

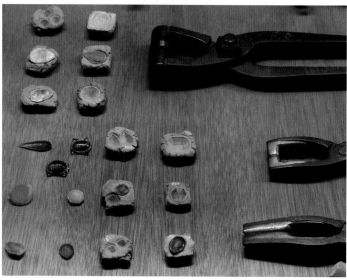

These are special pliers used for shaping pieces of hot glass into faceted cabochon shapes. They were used in the manufacturing of costume jewellery in North Bohemia. (From the collection of Museum of Glass and Jewellery in Jablonec nad Nisou, Czech Republic)

It is always helpful to have a good stock of stringers of various colours pre-made and ready.

how to form your beads or other lampwork you can have fun with decorating techniques. As with forming glass, decorating options are countless. Here it is really up to your imagination and taste as to what you create.

Stringers

These are long thin strips of glass. They can be bought from some manufacturers but they are easy enough to make; in that way you can have stringers made from all the colours of your rods and you can be sure that they will be compatible with them. Stringers are really helpful for decorating your work with stripes, lines, trails, small dots and other patterns. It is also a good way to use up pieces of your rods which are too small for bead work.

To pull a stringer you start by heating your glass rod in the same way as you would for making a bead. Then you grab the end of the molten glass with pliers or tweezers and start slowly pulling away. The pulled glass will form a thin string which will quickly harden in the air. The speed of your movements will determine the thickness of your stringers.

Frits

Frits are small pieces of glass which are used as a surface decoration. When melted onto the surface, they create small dots or specks of colour. If you heat them a little, they stay raised.

Decorating with stringers.

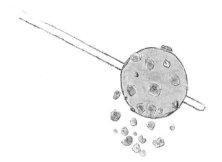

Beads with frits.

You can buy frits of different colours ready-made but, again, it is quite easy to make your own by crushing pieces of glass in a mortar. That way you can also control the size of the grains or create your own mixtures of two or more colours.

Thus you can recycle your own broken, unwanted pieces or small ends of rods. Just remember the compatibility rule.

Inclusions

If you want to introduce some metallic shine onto your work then try using metal foil. This is available in various shades – silver, copper or gold. If you do not want to invest in 24-carat gold foil then use one of the fake ones which look very similar.

You may want to experiment with thin metal mesh or thin metal wire. In case of the wire I would use 0.5mm thickness maximum to avoid the problem of internal stress of the glass during the cooling period. Borosilicate glass is much more suitable for insertion than soda-lime or lead glass because of its durability.

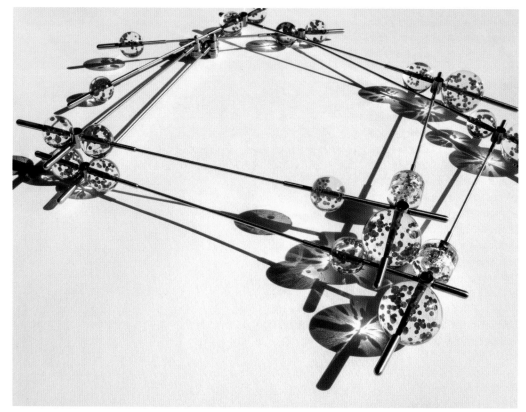

In *Rod Necklace* by Petr Dvořák we can see another interesting use of inclusion: Czech garnets are placed inside the layers of glass. He has used light titanium rods to construct the square frame and to secure the beads in place. (Photo: Petr Dvořák)

Baking powder is a simple ingredient which can help you achieve very interesting effects. You can use it in two ways. To create bubbles inside your glass piece, simply cover your base layer of glass with baking soda. Then enclose the whole bead in transparent glass. The soda will react in between the layers of your glass and make air pockets inside.

The other way of using baking powder is to achieve a 'weathered' look on your glass. When you look at ancient glass beads in the museums, they appear to have a matt, slightly crumbling surface. Even the transparent glass looks semi-opaque, a bit like sea glass. If you want your beads to look archaic or just different from other beads, just cover your finished bead in baking powder, heat it slightly and let it cool down. The powder will react with the surface of your bead.

Agustina Ros employs a fuming technique for her beautiful blown rings. She is uses gold and silver to create various shades and colours: 'My creative process begins at the torch. I work with both large and small flames, depending on the piece I want to perform. Blow and model. Then, I vaporize noble metals like gold and silver to dye the glass with shades that naturally fade.' (Photo: Agustina Ros)

Necklace created by Michelle Stewart using recycled found glass and applying lampworking. She has combined glass loops with silver and shibuichi links for the top part of the chain; this is both an aesthetically pleasing and a functional solution as glass loops would be too fragile to be placed on the more exposed neck area of the chain. (Photo: Andrew Barcham)

Fuming

Another interesting technique is to heat precious metals like silver or gold in the flame so that the metal vaporizes or 'fumes'. The microscopic particles are then cached and attached onto the surface of the glass, causing colour changes in the glass. Silver creates yellow/greenish shades, gold creates pink/reddish sheens.

Cold-Working

As with any other glass technique you can use cold-working techniques such as etching, faceting and sandblasting for your lampwork.

Etching and sandblasting are easy and effective ways of making the surface of your bead matted. You can also use it to hide any surface mistakes and impurities. It can be used for the whole surface or you can mask part of the bead and achieve contrasting surfaces. Remember that etching solution is an acid and it will work on metals as well so never insert your mandrels during this process.

You can use cold-working rotational tools to make facets or patterns on the surface of your glass. Polishing is not usually necessary with lampworking as you can always easily fire polish your pieces.

There is more detailed information in the following chapter.

COLD FORMING TECHNIQUES

In this chapter we will examine techniques which are used to manipulate, form or assemble glass which do not require any kilns, flame or other kind of heating equipment. We start with cold-working – methods of grinding, shaping and polishing your pieces of glass. This is really essential knowledge for anybody working with glass; you need to know how to finish your glass even if you are mostly using other techniques. Once you learn how to shape your glass you can then use cold construction to assemble your glass elements into new shapes. Then we look at metal foil technique which is used for assembling flat pieces of glass using metal frames. In the next part we look at how to use found glass elements, such as beach glass, and make them into jewellery pieces.

Cold-Working

As we said above, cold-working is the group of techniques used for shaping or finishing a piece of glass which do not include any heat processes – hence the name 'cold'. You may be working with raw glass material, found glass or a piece of glass you have already made with other techniques. Cold-working techniques are often required to finish a piece of jewel-

lery made with kiln forming techniques such as casting, especially to remove any sharp edges or misshaping. However, this set of techniques can be used alone to achieve the desired shape. Let's look at grinding, polishing, hand lapping and drilling.

Grinding and Polishing

These techniques will be easy to understand for jewellers who work with metals as the principle is similar. The difference is that glass is a much softer and more brittle material so slower,

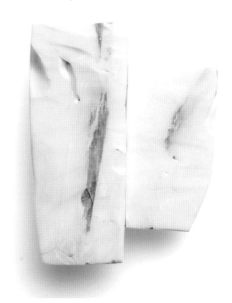

Emerging brooch by Federica Sala was made from carved glass cast with kyanite stones. (Photo: Federico Cavicchioli)

LEFT: ***Collier Rouge*** by Philip Sajet combines coloured glass with gold. (Photo: Philip Sajet)

diamond grinding equipment is used and water is needed during the whole process. Glass dust is a hazardous material and easily disperses into the air so it is necessary to keep your pieces wet all the time.

For removing material quickly you can use various grinding machines. There are specialist glass lathes and flat grinders which remove the material very quickly. On a glass lathe the wheel spins in the vertical plane (like a car wheel). The wheels are interchangeable and you can use various grades and profiles for different purposes. A flat grinder is a machine with a flat metal plate which spins horizontally. It has two kinds of plates: one which needs to be used with carborundum powders of different coarsenesses plus water; the other is a diamond wheel which doesn't require powder. The advantage of a lathe is that you can work on concave and convex shapes which would not be possible with a flat grinder. A constant supply of water is necessary for both lathes and grinders to lubricate the work.

The principles of grinding and polishing will be familiar to those who have experience with working with metal. You always start grinding with the roughest grade (220 grade is the most common but you can use 80 or 100 for rapid grinding) and progress towards the finest. For grinding you can use either carborundum powder or diamond surfaces of different grades. Carborundum is a hard mineral material (9 on the Mohs scale of hardness, similar to sapphire or ruby) and it acts as an effective abrasive. For a scratch-free polished finish, you need to progress through various grades – 320, 400 and 600 – slowly and thoroughly.

Make sure you cover the whole surface of your piece with each grade. To help you see where you have already worked the surface enough, there is a little trick. Cover the surface with permanent marker lines; once they disappear you can be sure you can continue with the next grade. Once you finish the 600 grade, you go to the finer, polishing stage.

For initial polishing, you use pumice powder (it is recommended that you use a cork wheel for this) and then progress to cerium powder on a felt wheel for the fine final polish.

Always remember to wash your piece, tools, hands, apron and anything else which could contaminate the next stage. It is really important to be patient and thorough with each stage as it is always disappointing if you find scratches in the later stages of your finishing; then you have to go back several stages to remove them.

You may choose to stop at earlier stages to achieve a translucent, matt effect on your piece. This finish would give your piece a different, I would say more ethereal, feel. Or you may choose to combine both effects – matt and highly polished transparent surfaces in one piece.

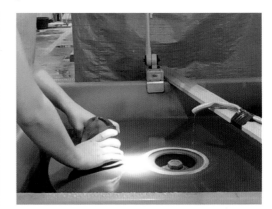

Lathe with diamond wheel; this is a very helpful tool which is particularly good for shaping rounded concave and convex shapes.

Flat bed grinder; the rotating round plate is exchangeable and is used with various grades of carborundum.

For jewellery use, a small bench-top grinder or lathe will be suitable, as shown here, although this could still be quite a significant expense. If you are just starting out with glass you can use smaller hand-held devices, such as a pendant drill or a Dremel with diamond grinding and polishing attachments.

The principle of grinding and polishing will be the same as with a flat bed or a lathe. You want to use your pendant drill on the lowest speed. It is very important to keep your piece of glass wet at all the time. It may be difficult have a constant dripping water supply as with the bigger machines but you can keep a container with water close by and regularly wash your piece. If you see white glass powder building up, you know it is time to rinse your piece. As you would be using electric devices you need to be very careful and make sure the water doesn't go inside the tool. You can isolate the weak points of your pendant drill with a layer of Vaseline or any other water-resistant material.

Another low-budget option would be to use carborundum grinding stones or diamond pads. These need to be used wet. It will take you a bit longer to grind material away as you will be using only the power of your hands but for small-scale jewellery this may be a suitable solution.

These processes are quite messy ones so make sure you use a waterproof apron and safety glasses. As with any rotational tool usage, make sure long hair is tied back and do not wear any long scarves, necklaces or headphones which could be entangled in the machine. Make sure you wash everything thoroughly before progressing to different grades to prevent contamination and scratches.

Hand Lapping

An alternative method of finishing your piece may be hand lapping, which is used for finishing flat surfaces or as a preparation for final polishing. This method would be suitable only for flat or faceted designs. For this process you

don't need any specialist machinery but it could be a little more time-consuming. On the other hand the slow removal of the material means that you are more in control. I enjoy it as it is this

This tabletop grinder is designed especially for flat sheets of glass used for fusing or metal foil techniques. The grinding element is quite small but efficient enough for jewellery purposes.

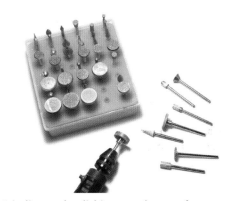

Grinding and polishing attachments for use with either pendant or hand-held drill.

Diamond pads; these come in different grades and are used by hand.

kind of repetitive, meditative kind of movement which makes me feel calm. For hand lapping you need a flat piece of float glass and carborundum grits (220, 320, 400, 600), pumice and cerium powders.

Place the piece of glass on newspaper to protect its surface and put the first carborundum grade mixed with water on the surface. Always start with the roughest grade of powder. Use a rotational movement to slowly grind your piece of glass down.

Continue through all the grades – 220, 320, 400 and 600. Finally, use pumice and cerium for a high polish. Make sure you use a different piece of float glass for each grade and wash your piece and your hands in between the stages.

Again, it is good to focus on each stage of the process. You can use permanent marker to help you see when the work on one stage is done, as previously described.

90 Degrees Rule

Glass doesn't like bevelling its edges – if the edges are too sharp then they have a tendency to chip. This can be quite frustrating when you are using cold-working techniques like grinding and hand lapping. However, there is an easy tip: just use a diamond pad or similar tool to round the edges slightly every time they go too sharp to prevent this happening.

Drilling Holes

You may be familiar with drilling so here are just a few tips on how to adjust your drilling technique to glass. For drilling holes in glass you need to use diamond drill burrs and drill bits, not the usual ones. Also, your piece needs to be wet all the time; keep lubricating it with water while working. Switch your drill to low speed to prevent breakages. While working, it is useful to check the progress of drilling from time to time and clear out the hole, especially with a thick piece. Don't try to drill the hole in one go; the slower you can drill, the better for the glass. Another trick to prevent your piece from chipping and breaking is to stop drilling when you are close to the other side. Turn your piece upside down and finish the drilling from the other side.

Cold Construction

Once you learn the basics of cold forming you may want to progress into constructing your pieces into more complex shapes. There is an interesting technique which combines decorative chemical bonding (gluing) with cold forming techniques to create surprising visual effects. I learned the basics of this technique from glass artist Martin Rosol. To achieve the best results it is best to use clear glass of optical quality, which means that there won't be any bubbles or other inclusions. The glass is cut into two or more sections which are then bonded together with a special glass glue mixed with pigments to achieve different coloured effects. The piece is then cold-worked into the final shape.

The finished pieces can then be mounted into jewellery pieces. Pavel Novák is another

Cold construction: first cut your pieces and bond them together with coloured glue.

artist who is using this technique at a smaller, jewellery scale.

Another approach to cold construction can be to use pre-made glass shapes and assemble them into various forms and settings, as in the work of Klára Mikešová. For the rings shown here, she has used thin lampworking rods and set bunches of them onto the silver ring settings.

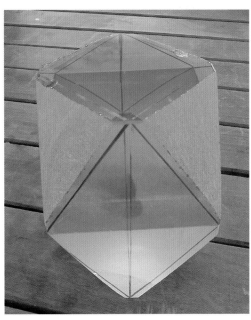

Then start to grind the edges; I use permanent marker to help measure the depth of the cuts.

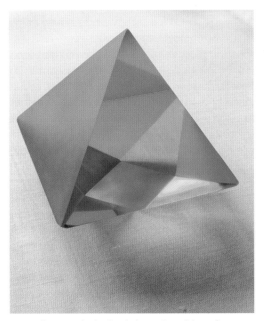

Once the rough desired shape is achieved, start to refine the surfaces by progressing through the various grades of polishing.

Then it is ready for final polishing. In this piece some of the facets stayed matt and some of them are highly polished, increasing the optical appeal. The finished piece appears either blue or transparent when viewed from different directions.

Origins rings, Klára Mikešová. This collection was designed using thin glass tubes, normally used just as a raw material for bead production. Instead, the artist took them in their original unprocessed state and created this unique piece of jewellery. Winner of the Preciosa Master of Crystal Award 2015. (Photo: Aleš Kosina, MSB)

David Mola's copper foil pendant and earrings. (Photo: David Mola)

Metal Foil

This technique, also known as 'Tiffany', is relatively new. It was invented by Louis C. Tiffany in the late nineteenth century and you may know it as the technique used for Art Nouveau mosaic lampshades. It involves using the principles of traditional stained glass construction but on a smaller scale. It is also suitable for creating three-dimensional shapes. This technique can be successfully used in jewellery to create either flat or sculptural shapes; the pieces have the characteristic metal rims between the glass panels.

For the metal foil technique you need some specialist equipment. You will need to cut flat sheets of glass so all the usual glass cutting tools will be needed. (Look back at the chapter on heat forming where glass cutting is described in detail.) For attaching the glass pieces together you need thin copper or other metal foil which you can obtain from specialist stained glass suppliers, plus a soldering iron with soft solder and flux.

Start by cutting the flat sheets of glass and wrap the edges with thin copper foil. The pieces can then be soldered together with soft solder, specifically low melting point solder; jewellery soldering equipment is not suitable for this process.

Follow the pictures to see the step-by-step process of

Pavel Novák uses the cold construction technique to its full potential in his cleverly designed rings. (Photo: Pavel Novák)

making the Leaf pendant, as designed and photographed by Edinburgh-based stained glass artist David Mola, who also specializes in the copper foil technique.

1. First, decide on the designs and shapes you want to use. It is best to start with simple shapes which are easy to cut.
2. Cut the glass into the required shapes, then grind and smooth down the edges. Clean every piece under running water to remove any glass dust left from the grinding which might prevent the copper foil sticking properly to the glass.
3. Next, apply copper foil by pressing it tightly around the edges. There are different types of copper foil; in this case David used black-coated $^7/_{32}$in.

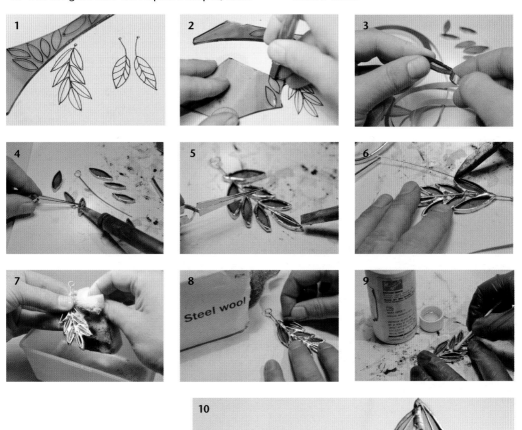

Making a copper foiled pendant. (Photo: David Mola)

4. Paint the entire copper surface with flux. You don't have to worry about flux running over your glass as this can be cleaned off afterwards.

5. The next step is soldering. Traditionally, solder is an alloy of tin and lead. On the market you can find different types of solder depending on the percentage of tin and lead. When this technique is used for wearable pieces which might be in contact with the skin, David recommends using lead-free solder.

    Solder every single piece of glass before joining them all together. Just apply a thin layer of solder all round your pieces. Do not forget the edges and the central wire which would hold all the pieces together! Then use that main central wire and solder each leaf to it one by one. Solder the back of your project to merge every leaf into one single piece.

6. Turn it back again and this time solder thinner pre-tinned wire running across every leaf.

7. Remember to clean your piece very well with soapy water. You need to get rid of all the remnants of flux; it is corrosive and will attack your foil if you do not clean it off properly.

8. Once it is dry, clean it thoroughly with 00 steel wool. This process will prepare the skin of the solder to take the patina.

9. Using protective gloves and cotton buds, apply the desired patina to the surface of the solder. You can choose between black finish and copper finish, or leave as it is, a silver colour. If you use patina, leave it work for 10 minutes and then clean it with a paper cloth. If you need a deeper colour, repeat the process.

10. And that is your copper foil leaf pendant finished!

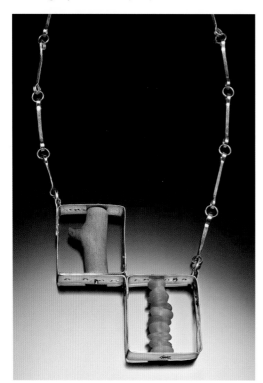

Two Squares necklace, Rex and Gene. This is a beach-themed necklace featuring beach glass and a piece of found wood. (Photo: Guy Nicol)

Square Peek a Boo Ring, Rex and Gene. (Photo: Guy Nicol)

Found Glass

Another approach to working with glass is to use found glass; this can be used in the form you found it or processed by using some of the cold-working techniques. We have already discussed this approach in the heat forming chapters of this book but from a different perspective.

You may want to incorporate existing glass objects like small bottles, glass sculptures or other flea market treasures into your jewellery. Many artists choose to use found beach glass for making their pieces: beach glass is already 'cold-worked' by exposure to elements and its usually small scale makes it perfect for jewel-lery use. It is really fascinating how the sea can change materials and force its own aesthetics upon them. Many of us love it because it re-calls good memories, the sense of peace and calmness when we spent time close to the sea. The only technical issue would be that beach glass requires some sort of attach-ment mechanism to be made into wearable items. Here are examples of what is possible to achieve with this material by artists Rex and Gene.

For a more edgy look you may want to consider using broken shards of glass. Here we have examples by jewellery artist Philip Sajet. The pieces are carefully set with gold wire to enhance the beauty of the glass itself.

Shards earrings, Philip Sajet. Both sides are equally striking. (Photo: Philip Sajet)

DECORATIVE TECHNIQUES

Even if you are making a very simple piece you can always add a unique quality to it by using one or more of the decorative techniques described in this chapter. We will start by exploring decorative techniques which use the removal of layers of material from the surface to create a pattern. There are many ways of achieving this: you can use hand or digital tools, chemicals or machinery. All of these techniques will work with the contrast of the surfaces – shiny and matt, raised and below the surface. The techniques explained here are engraving, laser engraving, sintering, etching and sandblasting.

Another set of techniques involve adding image and colour onto the surface of the glass: we look at painting, printing, decals and digital transfers.

Finally, we will look at techniques that use decoration on or inside the layers of glass, such as frits, stringers, metallic sheets and other inclusions. These are usually used in combination with kiln forming techniques such as fusing, or it may be possible to use cold bonding techniques such as lamination.

Altering the Surface

Engraving

Engraving is a mechanical way of removing a layer of glass from the surface of the piece, using a rotational tool or a machine with diamond wheels. The engraved layer will have a matt finish (unless you decide to polish it). You can achieve various depths depending on how much material you grind away. It could be a shallow relief and the difference between the engraved and non-engraved surfaces would be made more visible by contrasting finishes. You can achieve a more sculptural look with deeper engraving. You may be familiar with cameo jewellery with intricately engraved portraits and other miniature scenes portrayed in the stones or glass; these are fine examples of engraving in glass for jewellery but it would probably take you years to learn this skill. Start with something simple.

An engraving machine looks like a small version of a lathe. There are an exchangeable set of wheels which are attached to a rotating central spindle. The wheels need to be constantly lubricated with water to wash away the engraved glass powder, so some sort of water supply needs to be attached to the lathe.

It is a beautiful piece of equipment but if you only want to engrave small pieces of jewellery a pendant drill with a set of diamond bits would be enough. Just make sure you always have a container with water close to your working place to wash away the engraved glass powder building up on your piece. *It is essential to work carefully and methodically when using electrical*

LEFT: *Head in the Clouds* **necklace, Catarina Zucchi. (Photo: Chiara and Francesca Nicolosi)**

Traditional engraving lathe at The High School of Applied Arts for Glassmaking in Železný Brod, Czech Republic.

equipment near water. Dip only your piece of glass into the water, not the tool. To make sure you are safe you can cover any holes in your drill assembly with waterproof lubricant or electrical tape so no water can get in but be careful not to affect any ventilation.

Before you start engraving, make sure your glass is clean. You can draw or make guiding marks on the surface with permanent marker to help you manipulate your tool more precisely. Sometimes the engraving marks may be quite faint. Start by grinding shallow lines and gradually deepen the engraving. Each engraving tool will create a different mark on your glass so it is helpful to do a few tests on a scrap piece of glass first. Some tools are better at doing thin lines, some are good for removing larger fields of material. After a while you will see a white powder building up on your piece: this is a reminder to wash the glass.

Engraved identity bracelet, Klára Mikešová. This is from her *Identity* collection and is made from hand-blown uranium glass, hand-cut into the desired shape and then polished. The extraordinary lime colour of the glass is caused by a small addition of uranium, making the material glow in the dark under UV light, yet it is absolutely safe to wear. The hand-cut finish is inspired by the classic patterns used on Bohemian crystal glasses and beverage sets for centuries. Winner of the Preciosa Master of Crystal Award 2016. (Photo: Preciosa a.s.)

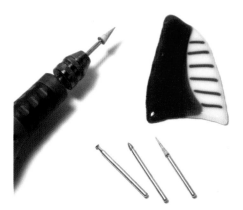

Small diamond bits can be used in a standard pendant drill for engraving pieces of jewellery.

Laser Engraving

This is a digital alternative to hand engraving. Instead of using mechanical rotational tools, the laser abrades the surface of the glass. This technique is great if you want engrave a photograph or a very detailed image onto your piece. It may be more cost-effective if you are mass producing or working on a bigger project. For this service contact a local or online engraving company to help you.

Sintering (Subsurface Laser Engraving)

This is a technology which allows you to engrave 3D forms inside a piece of glass: this makes it different from laser engraving which works only on the surface. It is used commercially for manufacturing awards, trophies, gifts and keepsakes – you have probably seen some of these before. Any two-dimensional image or photo, and to a certain degree a 3D image, could be reproduced by this process. This technique is a commercial one but I believe that it has a great potential for glass jewellery if it is used imaginatively. The glass needs to be of optical quality and transparency so that the engraving is visible. Again, this process requires specialist equipment so it is better to contact your local or online 3D engraver to discuss your project.

Etching

With this technique you can chemically remove material from the surface of your piece. The advantage of this method is that you don't need any specialist equipment apart from etching solution. You can try painting etching solution on the surface freehand but in most cases it is easier to use a protective layer to mask off the areas you want to leave shiny and raised. You can use some sorts of adhe-sive sheets, masking tape, a layer of washable acrylic paint or vinyl. You can cut the desired shape into the masking material by hand using a scalpel or scissors, or you may choose to use a laser cutter for more intricate designs. Laser cutting is especially suitable for vinyl material and in that way you can prepare a supply of many masking shapes in one go.

Once you have masked the areas which you want to protect, you apply etching solution on the open areas. There are different products on the market but probably the easiest solution on a small scale would be etching cream. You apply the cream onto the desired areas with a small brush and leave it for a couple of minutes, depending how deep you want your etching to be (the longer you leave the etching solution, the deeper the hole will be). Then rinse well. Make certain you follow the manufacturer's advice for your particular product.

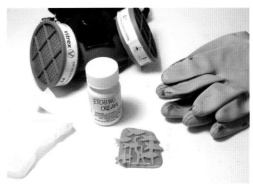

The etching process. Some areas are masked with tape and etching cream is carefully applied. After a few minutes, rinse the piece in water. Make sure you are wearing protective gloves and mask.

Be aware that any etching solution is a hazardous material so always wear protective gear, such as gloves and goggles, and thoroughly ventilate the work area. Do not use etching products if you are unwell or pregnant. Make sure the etching solution is stored somewhere safe in a labelled container, beyond the reach of animals or small children.

Sandblasting

As with etching, sandblasting means that you are removing material mechanically from the surface of the glass. Instead of using rotational tools for removal, this technique uses a machine which produces a stream of fine sand under pressure. The impact of the sand particles on the glass is such that the sand blasts away any uncovered surface. The principle of masking the areas you want to leave shiny is again similar to etching. The depth is easy to control and you can use a sandblaster even for making holes in your piece if you leave it exposed to the sand stream for long enough. Sandblasting leaves a really nice, even, satin finish. The surface could be a bit more sensitive for fingerprint marks than acid etching but the advantage would be that you are not using any chemicals in the process. A sandblasting machine could be

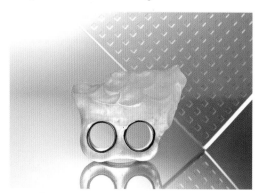

Ring, Özge Erbilen Yalçin. This is from her *Reflections of Tallinn* collection inspired by the city's architectural elements, urban texture and cultural influences. Here she is using cast glass finished with matt sandblasted surfaces. (Photo: Tolga Özdemir)

a significant expense but you may be able to access one in your local glass studio.

Decorating the Surface

Painting on Glass

There are many materials you can use to paint on glass. First, we look at the most durable option – glass enamels. These can be permanently fired onto the surface of your piece or fused inside the layers of transparent glass.

Enamels are basically very finely ground glass powders which can be mixed with water or another medium to paint onto glass. If you like painting generally then this may be a technique for you. Enamel colours can be transparent or opaque. Transparent ones leave a light, watercolour effect on your glass. If you want your paint to be thicker, let's say like acrylic paint, then use opaque colours. The colours may be different before and after firings so do some tests first.

There are low and high firing temperature enamels. Low firing ones need to be used as a last layer on a finished piece of glass. This piece can be heated only up to the low temperature – higher temperatures would burn the enamels. High firing temperature enamels can be used when you want to work with the glass further; for example, you have painted a piece of glass and want to fuse a layer of transparent glass over your painting. For the actual firing temperature of each product follow the manufacturer's advice as it differs brand to brand.

It is important to realize that you need to paint differently from how you work on paper. You may be working on a transparent piece so the light transmitted through your piece will have a significant effect on the appearance of your painted areas. The application of the colours onto the glass will vary depending on the enamel type. If you are using a powdered form, you need to mix your powder with water to create a smooth paste. You can add a little gum arabic or any other organic binder which will burn off in the kiln if you want to paint on an uneven surface. You may even choose to sift dry enamel powder onto the surface, with or without stencils.

Glass manufacturers always try to create new products for the market. You can now purchase a glass paint in handy squishy bottles or use glass paint pens for a fine line drawing. There is a big variety of different types of colours available on the market, including metallic, dichroic or pearl ones.

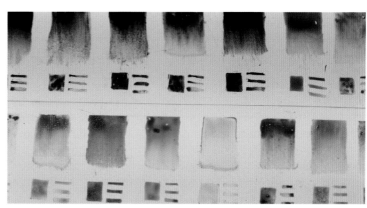

Creating an enamel test piece like this is a really helpful reference tool for your later practice.

Glass enamels are very similar to the jewellery enamels which are used on metals, so if you are already enamelling on metal you can experiment and use the same application techniques, such as sifting, stencils or print. However, the firing would need to be different, as you won't be able to use an enamelling kiln for glass.

Cold Paints

There is a wide variety of cold paint for glass: these may either be applied on glass cold without needing to be fired at all or some may need to be fired at kitchen oven temperatures. Cold paint is easy to use but it is not so durable and scratch-resistant as fired enamel paint. It can be a suitable option for pieces which are less exposed to touch, such as earrings.

Cold paint is a cheap and easy way of adding a layer of colour to your piece. The thicker the layer you paint, the less transparent it will appear. You can use this quality and combine transparent and opaque areas. These paints can be easily mixed and layered to create interesting effects. You can paint directly with brushes, use stencils, print with sponges and

Process of painting on glass. Mix your powdered enamels with water and carefully apply it on your piece. The enamels will change their appearance slightly after firing.

rubber stamps, doing pretty much anything you would be able to achieve with, say, an acrylic paint.

Printing on Glass

If you don't like freehand painting or are looking for a different effect you may want to try some printing techniques on your glass. The medium – enamels – would be the same. For printing purposes you would mix the enamel with a printing medium which will easily burn in the kiln without leaving marks: again, try gum arabic or wallpaper glue, or there are some specialist printing mediums – check with the manufacturer to see if they would be suitable for firing. Printing can then be done by simple rubber or potato stamps, patterns cut in lino or found objects such as leaves. You may want to explore more sophisticated printing techniques, such as screen print, which allows you to use even photographic images.

Transfers (Decals)

Transfers are an easy way of applying an image or photograph onto your piece of glass. (Transfers and decals are the same thing so when you search for the product, use both terms: here we will use the term 'transfer'.) There are two kinds

This statement piece by David Mola uses transfers of moths combined with gold leaf laminated in between the layers of float glass.

of transfers: permanent ones which are fired on and temporary ones which are applied to the surface of the glass cold. The permanent decals can then be high or low fired. Here we will talk only about permanent ones which use a screen-printed enamel image which is fired onto the surface of the glass.

You can buy ready-made transfers; glass suppliers have a wide variety of motifs in different colours or even metallic lustres. Look for fusing transfers specially formulated for glass application. The firing temperature is usually 730–800°C depending on your product.

If you want use your own images you can send them to be printed professionally (if you want full colour or lustre) or print your own. For this you would need special transfer papers and access to a black and white laser printer. In most cases, you can print your own transfers only in black and white. After firing, the black will then turn into a darker, sepia brown which can give your piece a satisfying vintage feel.

Here I will describe the process of applying a fired-on transfer but the process would be the same for all kinds of transfer. If you decide to use a cold transfer you would just let the piece dry and don't fire it at the end.

The image is printed in special enamel colours onto a gum-coated transfer paper. On the top of the enamel layer is a transparent overcoat which slightly overlaps your image. When you decide on your design, cut out the transfer of the image. You can use scissors, a scalpel or punches of different shapes. Then submerge it in water for a few minutes; the gum layer will dissolve and you will have your image slightly floating above the paper. The enamel print is very fragile at that moment so you need to be very careful not to damage it. Carefully slide the printed layer onto your glass and smooth it. Use a soft tool like a squeegee to help position your transfer correctly and carefully remove any excess water or bubbles from underneath the image. Let the piece dry (ideally overnight) and then fire it at the temperature recommended by the manufacturer. During firing, the transparent overcoat will be burned and your enamel will be left permanently fired onto your piece of glass.

This technique is relatively easy but it needs to be done carefully so the enamel print is not damaged. It allows you to use any image or photograph you want.

Other Possibilities

Decorating with glass powders, metal sheets, frits and stringers is especially suited for heat forming techniques such as fusing and lampworking. You can achieve all sort of stripy or dotted surfaces and contrasting colours. You can leave the decorations raised by choosing a lower fusing temperature or sink the elements into the mass of the glass with higher 'full fuse' temperature. The method of making your own stringers is described in the lampworking chapter of this book. It is essential that all the glass decorative elements you are using have the

Process of applying a metallic transfer to glass. Cut the pieces of transfers you intend to use and submerge them in water for a couple of minutes. Then slide the image on to your glass piece and let it dry. Metallic colour will appear after firing.

same CEO as your base glass, otherwise you are risking a breakage.

You may want to try decorating the surface of your glass with other materials such as fine wire work or heat-proof minerals; for example, mica is a beautiful shimmering material suitable for use with glass. Use only relatively small amounts of foreign material in the glass to avoid compatibility issues.

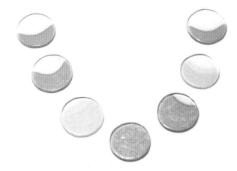

Surface decoration with silver leaf, which turns to shimmering gold/yellow after being fused onto the surface of the glass.

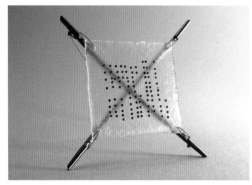

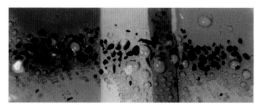

Bubble inclusions: this is a fused test piece with the bubble and black frit inclusions visible.

Cross IV, Petr Dvořák. Czech garnets are fused on the surface of the glass, instead of inside as with Petr's other works featured in this book. The brooch is finished with a dramatic titanium backing. (Photo: Petr Dvořák)

Inclusions

Another visually exciting property of glass is that it is able to trap other materials as inclusions in between its layers. These can be done by heating the layers and trapping the material permanently or by the cold technique called lamination. This can be particularly useful for jewellery as it allows some interesting possibilities of how to attach the findings.

The decorative possibilities of using various objects inside transparent glass are endless. You can use metal wires, metal leaf, enamels, fibre-glass, small beads, sections of glass rods or scrap from your metal jewellery making; for example, silver or gold filings fused between the layers of transparent glass create very interesting effects. You can buy special coloured fusing papers and inclusion pens from glass suppliers.

Adding intentional air bubbles to your piece can look very beautiful. You need to create pockets of air between the pieces of glass before the firing. There are several way of doing this: for example, you can arrange your pieces in such a way that, when melted, air bubbles are sealed inside the glass mass. You can work with wire or drill or sandblast the holes at specific places. You can also try trapping a little baking soda in between the layers to create larger air bubbles – this would be my favourite method.

This process is open for your own experimentation – you can try inserting ceramic glazes, sands and so on. But you also need to be careful: glass is capable of accepting only a certain

Deborah Timperley has used 23.5-carat gold inclusions in her cast black and clear glass necklace. Gold keeps its colour and lustre through the firing and makes a distinctive contrast with the black layer underneath. (Photo: Deborah Timperley)

Sugar Cane brooch, Lisa Johnson. Lisa employs an experimental approach to her fused pieces with surprising inclusions. This one is fabricated in soldered sterling silver with tube set stones and a large prong-type setting for the glass. The glass piece consists of two layers of glass with a slice of sugar cane fired in between. Instead of a print or fossil left behind, parts of the sugar remain captured in the glass. (Photo: Lisa Johnson)

percentage of its own volume. I would strongly advise you to do tests before using inclusions in your final piece.

Always have your kiln ventilation open when using inclusion in case any unwanted burning happens – this could contaminate your pieces.

Lamination

Lamination is basically a way of gluing two pieces of glass together. It is a cold technique, so you can use any sort of inclusions which wouldn't be suitable for heat processes. It is really effective for any flat inclusions such as dried leaves, drawings, cut-outs from magazines and similar items. For gluing the pieces together it would be the best to use a strong, stable and transparent kind of glue: you can choose from epoxy, silicon, resin or UV glues.

The method is quite straightforward. Make sure both of the pieces of the glass are clean. Apply the glue evenly across one part of the glass and then apply the inclusions. Then you spread the second layer of glue evenly over the glass and inclusions, and stick both parts of the glass together. It may be helpful to put some sort of flat weight (like a pile of books) on the top of the drying lamination to make sure the glue dries evenly.

The challenge of this technique is dealing with the sides of your laminated pieces. If you are lucky, the sides may look quite tidy but in most cases they will not. You may consider some ways of hiding the edges, such as framing, bezel setting or wrapping them in copper foil.

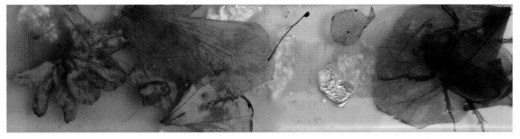

Example of lamination by David Mola: pieces of dried leaves are combined with acetone prints and metal foil.

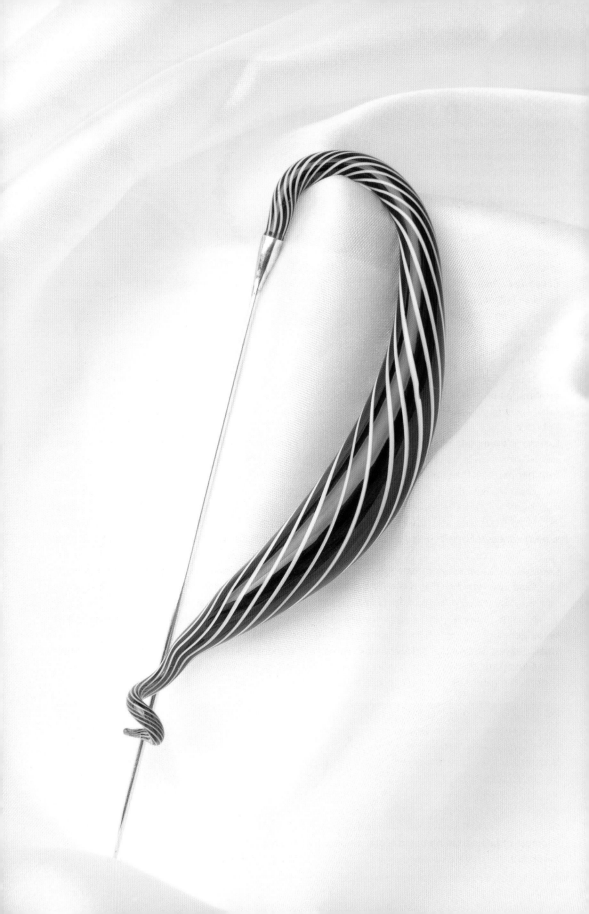

FURTHER READING

Beveridge, Philippa; Domenech, Ignasi; Pascual, Eva. *Warm Glass: A Complete Guide to Kiln-Forming Techniques: Fusing, Slumping, Casting* (Us Imports, 2008)

Blackson, Robert; Davies, Peter. *Glass North East* (Arts Editions North, University of Sunderland, 2007)

Brown, Sarah; O'Connor, David. Medieval Craftsmen: *Glass Painters* (British Museum, 1991)

Coffey, Yvonne: *Glass Jewellery* (A. & C. Black, 2010)

Cummings, Keith. *Contemporary Kiln-Formed Glass* (A. & C. Black, 2009)

Cummings, Keith. *Techniques of Kiln-Formed Glass* (A. & C. Black, 1997)

Cutler, Vanessa. *New Technologies in Glass* (A. & C. Black, 2012)

Gear, Alan D.; Freestone, Barry. *The Complete Guide to Glass Painting: Over 80 Techniques with 25 Original Projects and 400 Motifs* (Collins & Brown, 2001) (later edns available)

Griffith, Brenda. *Beginner's Guide to Kiln-Formed Glass* (Lark, 2012)

Griffith, Brenda. *Kiln-Formed Glass: Beyond the Basics* (Lark, 2014)

Ilse-Neuman, Ursula; Holzach, Cornelie; Page, Jutta-Annette. *GlassWear: Glass in Contemporary Jewelry* (Arnoldsche Art, 2007)

Jargstorf, Sibylle. *Glass in Jewelry: Hidden Artistry in Glass* (Schiffer, 1991)

Jenkins, Cindy. *Making Glass Beads* (Lark, 1998)

Lundstrom, Boyce; Schwoerer, Daniel. *Glass Fusing: Book One* (Vitreous, 1983)

Papadopoulos, George. *Lamination (Glass Handbooks)* (A. & C. Black, 2004)

Persico, Jayne. *Innovative Adornments: An Introduction to Fused Glass and Wire Jewelry* (Wardell, 2002)

Petrie, Kevin. *Glass and Print* (A. & C. Black, 2006)

Schuler, Frederic; Schuler, Lilli. *Glassforming: Glassmaking for the Craftsman* (Pitman, 1971)

Schwarzinger, Veronika; Šibor, Jiří. *Glass in Czech Jewelry* (exh. cat.) (Vienna, Brno, Prague, 2009)

Tait, Hugh. *Five Thousand Years of Glass* (British Museum, 1991)

Tettinger, Corina. *Passing the Flame: A Beadmaker's Guide to Detail and Design* (Bonzobucks & Books, spiral edn, 2002)

Thwaites, Angela. *Mould Making for Glass* (Bloomsbury, 2011)

Watkins-Baker, Helga. *Kiln Forming Glass* (Crowood, 2010)

Notes

[1]Tait, H., *Five Thousand Years of Glass* (British Museum, 1991), p.21.

[2]Tait, *Five Thousand Years of Glass*, p.23.

[3]Cummings, K., *Tecchniques of Kiln-Formed Glass* (A. & C. Black, 1997).

[4]Tait, *Five Thousand Years of Glass*, p.8.

LEFT: ***Nightingale Eye*** brooch, Özge Erbilen Yalçin. (Photo: Tolga Özdemir)

INDEX